PENGUIN BOOKS

SHOOT. DIVE. FLY.

Rachna Bisht Rawat is the author of six books published by Penguin Random House India, including the bestsellers *The Brave* and *Kargil*. She lives in Gurugram with Hukum, the bright-eyed, bushy-tailed golden retriever; an eclectic collection of books and music; and Manoj Rawat, the man in olive green who met her when he was a gentleman cadet at the Indian Military Academy and offered to be her comrade for life. Occasionally, they are visited by Saransh the Wise, who has moved out to explore the world on his own. She can be reached at www.rachnabisht.com and rachnabisht@gmail.com. Her Instagram handle is @rachna_bishtrawat.

RACHNA BISHT RAWAT
Foreword by M.S. Dhoni

SHOOT.
DIVE. FLY.

PENGUIN BOOKS

An imprint of Penguin Random House

PENGUIN BOOKS

USA | Canada | UK | Ireland | Australia
New Zealand | India | South Africa | China | Singapore

Penguin Books is part of the Penguin Random House group of companies
whose addresses can be found at global.penguinrandomhouse.com

Published by Penguin Random House India Pvt. Ltd
4th Floor, Capital Tower 1, MG Road,
Gurugram 122 002, Haryana, India

First published in Penguin Books by Penguin Random House India 2017

30 29

The views and opinions expressed in this book are the author's own and the
facts are as reported by her which have been verified to the extent possible,
and the publishers are not in any way liable for the same.

ISBN 9780143428671

Typeset in Adobe Caslon Pro by Manipal Digital Systems, Manipal
Printed at Gopsons Papers Pvt. Ltd., Noida

www.penguin.co.in

For my father, Brigadier B.S. Bisht,
SM, VSM—the bravest soldier I've ever known,
even though he has now gone beyond the realm of books.

Contents

Foreword   xi

Introduction   xv

Hanging by a Thread

1. 'I fly a helicopter to work.'   3
2. 'I shouldn't have been alive.'   15
3. 'She was stuck thirty feet underground in
   a narrow borewell.'   29
4. 'We aimed for zero collateral damage.'   39

In Extremis

5. 'Jumping out of a plane makes me feel alive!'   53
6. 'My missing finger is my mountaineering
   trophy.'   65
7. 'We could have died on that expedition—but
   we didn't.'   75

Contents

8. 'On Everest, mental fortitude counts more than physical strength.'   84

The Incredibles

9. 'Everything in my body is broken—except my smile!'   101

10. 'I hit the ground from 8,500 feet with an unopened parachute.'   112

11. 'They were hanging between life and death when he dropped down from the sky.'   121

12. 'I chopped off my leg with my own khukri.'   128

13. 'When you have nothing to lose, there is no fear.'   139

Training to be a Soldier

14. 'At twenty-five, you will lead a 100 men ready to die at your command.'   151

15. 'I play troop games like football; I can shoot from a rifle and I know unarmed combat—every lady officer does.'   162

16. 'I stood in the snake pit watching the cobra come closer.'   169

Popular Myths Busted

17. 'It's not a career for women!'   183

18.	'It's a no-brain job!'	195
19.	'It grounds your dreams of going abroad.'	203
20.	'I joined the Army at forty.'	211
21.	'There's no promotion for disabled soldiers.'	217

Institutions   223

How Do I Join the Army?   231

Acknowledgements   235

Foreword

My dear friends,

It gives me great pleasure to write the foreword for *Shoot. Dive. Fly*. The Indian Army is one of the most respectable and exciting careers our country offers young people and it surprises me that the Army faces a shortage of officers year after year. This is probably because most of us do not know what an amazing variety of jobs it offers. Perhaps this is also because Army officers are not permitted to talk to the media and so we never get to hear about the amazing things they do. I compliment the Army on giving Rachna Bisht Rawat access to young serving officers to share with us the experiences of the fascinating jobs they do.

This book will help bust the false belief that an Army officer is a man with a gun who lives on the borders of the country, cut off from the rest of civilization, waiting for a war to begin, which might sound like a boring job to a lot of teenagers. They do that, of course, and we are very proud of them for it, but that's not the whole truth. Army officers do a lot of other things too that most teens want from a career. The Army has engineers, doctors, helicopter pilots, drone fliers, cyber warriors, Olympians, Everest summiteers, skydivers, sailors, marathon runners, shooters—and yes, even cricketers—and a host of other professionals that we often don't get to hear about. These are men and women who are all trained for combat but they work in their particular fields with all the support of the Indian Army to reach the top. You, too, can choose one of these opportunities and get paid to be trained and excel in your dream job. Not many, if any, industries or institutions give you this freedom. And how do I know all this? Because I happen to be an officer in the Indian Territorial Army too.

I am sure you will enjoy reading the real-life stories of young officers who went beyond the ordinary to reach great heights. This book includes the story of Colonel Ivan J. Crasto, SC, who climbed down a rope from a hovering helicopter to rescue all ten tourists trapped on board a trolley hanging from a snapped wire. It also tells of Colonel Rajesh Unnikrishnan who climbed down forty feet into a dark, gaping borewell to rescue a small child who had fallen in. In these pages, you will meet Colonel Sameer Singh Bisht, SM, whose gun jammed in an encounter with Kashmiri terrorists but he managed to keep his nerve and emerge victorious. You will read of young mountaineer Major Deepika Rathore, who has climbed the mighty Mount Everest twice and of my fellow paratrooper Major Sandesh Kadam, who jumped out of a plane at 8,500 feet to find that both his main and emergency parachutes would not open. How did he land alive and undamaged in spirit to the extent that he is raring to recover completely and go back to his duty, you might ask? To know that, you will need to read this book, and/or join the Army.

I shall sign off by wishing you the best in whatever career you choose. When I am old and sitting in front of the TV watching some of you play cricket for India, or some of you do amazing things that the news channels report, I shall smile and applaud for you—just like you do for me, when I hit a six or take a catch. I shall be proud of all of you. Go on and do your best in life. But do consider wearing the uniform once before you make a final choice. I did!

Jai Hind! Jai Hind ki Sena!

Lieutenant Colonel Mahendra Singh Dhoni

Introduction

Dear reader,

As I write to you from a shaded corner of my lawn, lounging on my red beanbag, my book finally finished, spring has sprung upon Delhi Cantonment. The birds are chirping, bright-pink bougainvillea blossoms are sprouting and Huzoor, our huge two-year-old Golden Retriever, is lying on his back, trying to get an upside down view of the world. Michael Jaikisan, our resident dancing peacock with the long, shimmering tail, is perched on the gate, watching Huzoor's lack of dignity with undisguised disgust.

Believe it or not, this beautiful oasis exists in the middle of dusty, polluted Delhi, where at this very moment, the roads are jammed with screeching, honking, poison-spewing vehicles. A quiet, peaceful, tree-lined residence is just one of the perks that the Army gives you. The others are plush gymnasiums, Olympic-sized swimming pools, squash and tennis courts, swanky schools that don't demand donations, state-of-the-art hospitals, plush Messes, open-air cinema halls and—the most precious of all—friends for life.

I have spent all of my forty-seven years (I'm afraid I'm ancient!) in various Army cantonments across the country. My dad was in the Army (so is my husband!) and believe me, it is a beautiful world unparalleled by anything I see outside. It always surprises me that more kids don't look at the Army as a viable career. 'It's probably because they don't know much about it,' I used to tell myself. And so, when Penguin Random House decided to do a book about the Indian Army, and editor Sohini Mitra offered the job to me, I was happy to write it.

This book is meant to introduce you to the whole universe that the Army actually is, which is often one that people outside don't really know exists. Did you know that the Army is a career that lets you do things like skydiving, rally driving, mountaineering, flying a helicopter to work while you are on the job? You get paid to do things you'd like to pay for—and often even those chances never arise.

This book will tell you what Army officers actually do through the stories from the lives of twenty-one Army officers. You might just discover that they are living out some of your favourite fantasies. They weren't difficult to find; the fact is that every Army officer has an interesting story to tell, but since they are not supposed to talk about their work and missions, we never get to hear about these adventures. This is the first time Indian soldiers have shared what they do because the Indian Army came forward and generously gave us permission to interview young officers—something they have never done for a book before. I hope that you will find some of these stories thrilling, some nail-bitingly unbelievable, some might make you chuckle, others might fill you with the desire to jump out of a plane with a parachute on your back or maybe fly a helicopter over the Siachen Glacier. I'll admit as well—I am very much hoping that these stories will make some of you want to be a part of the Indian Army.

If that happens, don't hesitate. Just step across the invisible line that separates the magical folk in olive-greens from the rest of the world; the Army waits to envelop you in its warm group hug. All it asks from you in return is a fit body, a brave heart, a healthy mind and the capacity to live life to its fullest.

Do you have it in you?

Rachna Bisht Rawat

Hanging by a Thread

What's a day in the Indian Army like?

You could fly a chopper to work, keep a gun handy, row across a freezing lake to attack a terrorist camp or climb down a gaping hole to rescue a child—and it's all in a day's work. You never get bored!

1

'I fly a helicopter to work.'

Lieutenant Colonel Anupam Gaur, of the Army Aviation Corps, shares what being a helicopter pilot in the Army is all about and describes a miraculous chopper rescue he was part of.

6 October 2007
At 19,000 feet
Somewhere in the Siachen Glacier

Snow has started falling when the Cheetah helicopter reaches the frozen heights. The young pilot looks out at the vast sea of white, his eyes desperately searching for the missing mountaineers. He knows he cannot land in the soft snow. And also that he has very little time. If he runs out of fuel he will have to return, reducing further the adventurers' chances to live. Keeping his nerves steady, he hovers above the sloping glacier, the helicopter's rotor blades kicking up a cloud of snow. Every passing second reduces the possibility of rescue. It is then that his co-pilot draws his attention to some blurry shapes moving towards them in the haze. 'It's them!' he whispers. Even in that moment of extreme stress, the two of them look at each other and smile.

They watch breathlessly as the mountaineers come into their line of vision. They are trying their best to reach the chopper as fast as they can. The two Army Aviation Corps pilots know that, out of the team of eleven mountaineers, one has a broken shoulder, another an ankle fracture and two have developed frostbite. They have attempted this rescue a day earlier too, but have had to fly back since there was no place to land. The plan today is to hover over the ground and pull in the mountaineers, one at a time, take each down to a safe location, and return for the next. The chopper is on mininum fuel to lessen its weight, so that it is easier to control, which is another reason why the rescue has to be quick since the machine can crash if it runs out of fuel.

The first mountaineer reaches the chopper, lean and haggard, his face streaked with tears, and is pulled up by the co-pilot, amidst sighs of relief from the others. Major Anupam Gaur flies off into the air, promising to return. He does three trips that day and manages to take three of the mountaineers back to safety. Between the three helicopters on the rescue mission that cold day in Siachen, they save the lives of all eleven members of the stranded team.

* * *

When I meet forty-four-year-old tall, dark and good-looking Anupam Gaur, now a Lieutenant Colonel, ten years have passed since that daredevil rescue in Siachen. With aviators shading his eyes, he looks more like a movie star than the young pilot who helped save three lives on that freezing October day. Tell him that and he gets really embarrassed.

'I'm not a hero—I'm just a regular guy in the Army. That rescue is one of the most precious memories of my life but it is nothing extraordinary if you look at a career in uniform. Army officers do these things all the time. I can bet you that no other profession can match what we do for a living,' he says. 'I fly a helicopter for a living—I've dropped skydivers off at 10,000 feet. I've chased lions in an African national park, my chopper hovering twenty feet above the ground while on a UN mission. I've flown fellow officers around, including Lieutenant Colonel Mahendra Singh Dhoni from the Indian Territorial Army,' he quips with a wide smile while adding, 'You might have heard of him—he also plays cricket.'

If he's asked to express in one word what the Army has given him, Gaur says the answer would be 'everything'. His journey began when he cleared the National Defence Academy (NDA) entrance exam at eighteen and took a train to Pune to join the academy.

'We were a bunch of thin, scruffy young boys nervous about what lay ahead but the moment we reached the Academy, we were lined up for haircuts and given an NDA blazer each. And overnight, without doing a thing, we became local heroes. When we went out, girls would look at us and it was a nice feeling,' he laughs.

Besides regular academics, the three years at NDA taught Gaur swimming, boxing, horse riding, football, handball, martial arts and also had him going on ten-kilometre cross-country runs regularly. Learning a foreign language was compulsory so he picked German. Table manners were taught by a senior who sat next to him at meal times for a year and from whom he learnt stuff like keeping his elbows off the table while eating, and using the right fork and knife for each course. After a year, Gaur had learnt enough to sit next to his own understudy (a fresher) and teach him the same things. 'We also attended parties where we would be given the opportunity to sit alongside ladies, mostly the wives of our instructors. That's how we were taught to pull out chairs and open doors for ladies, be attentive to them and pick up other nuances of chivalrous behaviour.'

The Academy even had a ballroom dancing club where dances would be organized and girls from local colleges would be invited as partners for the cadets. 'The Academy reinvented us completely. It taught us to walk smartly, talk confidently, address gatherings and learn self-defence. Boys who were non-swimmers became swimmers, some like me who had never been near a horse became riders, some developed a passion for sailing and yet others went on to become boxers and shooters. Knowing how to do so many things made us really confident,' he says. 'We came out of the Academy feeling like supermen, we felt there was nothing that we couldn't do and we had the moral responsibility and more importantly, the strength and training, to stand up for our country and our principles in times of need. I'm sure that even the best university in the world cannot give you so much in one package,' he says.

First posting at the Siachen Glacier

Gaur's first posting as a twenty-two-year-old was at the Siachen Glacier. He remembers, 'I was sent to Amar, a post at 20,000 feet, where breathing was difficult due to the thin air. That is where I saw Army Aviation Corps pilots with their Cheetah helicopters dropping down from the sky and I was completely awestruck. They would take us to the post, landing there despite heavy shelling from the Pakistani side. Then, with a cheerful wave, they would fly off, ignoring the Pakistani fire completely. Nothing seemed to scare them. Every few days they would return with medicines, rations and letters for us. They would evacuate sick men and bring reinforcements and for me they became instant heroes. Flying a helicopter at the highest altitude in the world, supporting your own men in uniform was glamorous work and that was what I wanted to do.'

After three years of service, Gaur volunteered for the Army Aviation Corps. He was selected and landed in the Air Force Academy in Dundigal near Hyderabad. 'For the first six months, we were trained on fixed-wing training aircraft along with Air Force cadets. Wearing blue overalls, flying solo, learning about the system of the aircraft, interacting with fighter pilots who had amazing stories to tell, who would tell us how it felt to break the sound barrier—all these were amazing new experiences for us,' Gaur recounts nostalgically. 'From a ground soldier who did route marches with a rifle and backpack, I had suddenly become airborne. Of course, I didn't think of it then but the cost of training to be a pilot is Rs 30 to 50 lakhs outside and we were doing it for free. In fact, we were also getting paid a salary. Our evenings would be free—we would eat out, attend parties and meet people. We were doing the same kinds of things any other youngster our age would be doing outside the Army—plus a lot more.'

After six months, the officers were shifted to helicopters, and were trained for a year on the five-seater light combat Cheetahs, which hold the record for high-altitude flying amongst all categories of helicopters, and the seven-seater Chetaks, which are used for cargo transport, casualty evacuation, and search and rescue operations. Now, of course, the Army also has the state-of-the-art Dhruv helicopters which are multi-engine glass cockpit aircrafts. After the training was complete, Gaur was posted to Udhampur in Jammu and Kashmir. 'It was a great feeling to be alone in the cockpit. We used to memorize the Line of Control, do fuel calculations and often take loads to posts on the border in bad weather conditions and low visibility. It was a new experience.'

Chasing lions in Africa

Another incident that Lieutenant Colonel Gaur shares is his experience in the United Nations Peacekeeping Forces in the year 2005–06.

'Our unit was sent to the Democratic Republic of Congo as part of a UN Peacekeeping Force. When you go on missions like these the boundaries of being from different countries blur. All of us are soldiers who wear the UN uniform and the light blue UN beret. Our salary shoots up in those tenures since the UN is paying that to our country.

'When we went to Congo, supporting a division (headed by a General from Senegal) with three brigades comprising Indians, Bangladeshis and Pakistanis. There was a 'surgical strike' across the Sudan border, quite like in the movies where commandos were inserted before first light and extracted as soon as the operation is completed.'

'I had the opportunity to be a part of that stealth operation,' he says. While in Congo, Gaur also had the opportunity to fly in countries like Rwanda, Uganda, Tanzania and the Republic of Congo. 'Interacting with their people, flying over their terrain was an enriching experience,' he says.

He recounts for me an incident when he was flying his chopper from Goma to Beni to recce some militant camps that had to be destroyed. Flying over the Virunga National Park, known for the glaciated Rwenzori Mountains—also knowns as the Mountains of the Moon—the conversation with his fellow officers veered to how they frequently spotted herds of wild elephants and buffaloes but had never seen a lion so far.

'Even as I said this, an officer on board shouted out that he could spot a lion below. He directed us to turn the chopper and fly lower. Hovering just twenty-five feet above the ground, we saw a big beautiful African lion with a magnificent golden mane trying to figure out who or what we were. Startled by our whirring wings, he ran! We followed him for a while till he hid behind a bush. We then hovered lower, clicked some pictures, waved him a respectful goodbye and went on our way. I also remember an incident when we were flying over a herd of elephants. Just for fun, I lowered the chopper and hovered before them. It was fascinating to see how the alpha male, with his complete herd behind him, lifted his trunk, flapped his big ears and took an attack stance even as our helicopter took off and left. These are experiences I shall treasure all my life.'

The Siachen rescue

Gaur talks to me about that amazing helicopter rescue he was part of in Siachen in the year 2007, when he was posted there soon after his Congo tenure. 'We were at the base camp, where three Army Aviation and four Air Force helicopters would be parked, on standby for emergencies. We lived in fibreglass huts and there was twenty-four-hour electricity. Every morning, we would be up at 5.30 a.m. to sort out what supplies needed to be carried to which post. If a soldier had taken ill at a post, we would help evacuate him. If medicines needed to be dropped off somewhere, we would do that too. It was a very satisfying job since we were supporting our own men.'

Around 22 September 2007, the base camp had some visitors. These were seasoned mountaineers on an expedition. They were on their way to Rimo, one of the toughest peaks to climb. At 24,229 feet, it is one of the highest Himalayan peaks in India, located in the north-east of the subcontinent, in the Siachen Glacier, where the borders of all three countries—India, China and Pakistan—meet. 'They were taking an off-route track to the summit which was not a good idea since the weather was turning bad. We advised them not to go but they were adamant and so we saw them on their way.'

Nearly ten days after the team had left, Gaur was sitting in his fibreglass hut wondering why the expedition had not returned when he got a satellite call through the Leh exchange. The expedition leader was on the other end. He told Gaur that during the final climb, the ropes securing the mountaineers had broken and the entire team had taken a nasty fall. Three members were badly injured, and the rest were also in bad shape. The team needed to be evacuated immediately since they had run out of food. 'I have just two minutes of phone battery left, we are near the final summit. If you don't come and rescue us, we will all die here,' the expedition leader told him.

Necessary permissions were sought and obtained at once for the rescue, food packets loaded into the helicopters and the pilots took off. 'It took us nearly an hour to locate them in the snow; they were stranded at 19,000 feet,' says Gaur. They dropped food packets to the climbers but most were lost in the snow. The mountaineering team managed to communicate with the chopper crew and told them that one climber's shoulder had broken, another had an ankle fracture and two people had developed frostbite. They were in no condition to walk and the choppers would have to come and rescue them from where they were. Since there was no place to land, the helicopters had to return and one more day lapsed. The next morning, the pilots took off again, this time with a do or die spirit, flying on minimum fuel to lessen aircraft weight so that it was lighter and easier to control. The pilots swooped down over the climbers. Hovering barely a foot above the ground, since they couldn't land on the soft snow, the plan was that the pilot would keep the chopper steady while the co-pilot would pull the injured people into the machine.

'The weather was really bad that day. The helicopter rotors were kicking up freshly fallen snow. It was too soft for us to risk a landing so we flew close to the ground, looking out for the missing mountaineers. It was a moment of great elation when the first mountaineer managed to climb into the hovering helicopter. It was as if life had won,' remembers Gaur.

All eleven members were rescued and evacuated to Leh where an IL-76 aircraft was waiting to take them to New Delhi immediately. They were admitted to the Army Research and Referral Hospital and all of them survived. Some had lost fingertips to frostbite but it was a small price to pay for being alive. 'When you face situations like these, you surpass your own limitations. I would have never believed that we could have hovered there in the falling snow with one skid on the ground and the other in the air, but we did it. Our only concern at that time was to save their lives, and we managed to do it,' he says, nostalgia clouding his eyes.

There's no better life

Gaur says there is no better life than being in the Indian Army. 'I was a cadet at eighteen and an officer at twenty-two. From an absolute nobody, the Army shaped me into a soldier, a flier, an instructor, an adventurer, an officer and a gentleman. It helped me to see the world, gave me the confidence to walk into any situation, be it a party or a war zone. If I had to convince a youngster about joining the Army I would say it gives you a starting pay package of Rs 1.5 lakhs a month cost to company, which is comparable to the best starting job opportunity in the world. What's more is that it ensures you will never be bored in the rut of a nine-to-five job,' he says.

'You have complete flexibility about what you want to do. You can be a ground soldier, a doctor, an engineer, a pilot, a skydiver, a rallyist or a sailor. You can participate in adventure sports, play golf all your life and climb mountains. From the very first day you go to work in your uniform, there are people waiting to take orders from you. And yes, of course, ladies tend to get impressed with your work clothes.' With that parting shot, Lieutenant Colonel Anupam Gaur, recipient of two commendation cards from the Army Chief and one from the General Officer Commanding, Northern Command, puts on his aviator shades, flashes me a Tom Cruise smile, and drives off into the mad din of Delhi. His faithful helicopter probably waits for him somewhere.

The Army Aviation Corps

If you would like to join the Indian Army and be a helicopter pilot, you might like to consider opting for the Army Aviation Corps. It is a component of the Indian Army that is headed by a Director General of the rank of Lieutenant General at the Army headquarters, New Delhi.

The freezing snow-covered Siachen Glacier has been one of the toughest operational grounds of the Army Aviation

Corps. Routinely operating at 20,000 feet and above is not easy but the Cheetah helicopter has been doing it routinely, thus proving itself to be the workhorse of the glacier. The Army Aviation Corps has been responsible for saving hundreds of lives besides providing logistic support at those high altitudes where surviving is a challenge by itself. It is a feat unparalleled by any other Army in the world.

The Army Aviation Corps is involved in challenging tasks like combat search and rescue, artillery lifts, combat transportation, military prisoner transportation and medical evacuation. Their pilots do this not just in war or war-like situations but also during natural calamities like floods or earthquakes. Their choppers also sustain life in border posts in the North-east that get cut off from civilization during bad weather conditions by dropping off food and medical supplies. Pilots for the Corps are picked up from all arms with young officers volunteering to join. All Army Aviation pilots are trained at the Combat Army Aviation Training School at Nasik.

2

'I shouldn't have been alive.'

Colonel Sameer Singh Bisht, SM, PARA, one of the battalions from The Parachute Regiment, recounts a Kashmir operation where he and his men risked their lives to hunt down twenty terrorists who had crossed the Line of Control with a big stock of weapons.

The Kashmir encounter

23 September 2003
Baraub, North Kashmir

Dusk is falling. The pale yellow glow of the setting sun lights up two soldiers with AK-47s in their hands. Tall, hefty, hook-nosed Subedar Bhim Singh Raizada has a menacing scowl and narrow piercing eyes. His company commander, short, slim, large-eyed Captain Sameer Singh Bisht looks gentle and harmless till you notice his smashed boxer nose. The two of them have been dropped by helicopter on a freezing

18,000-foot-high ridge along with a team of forty-two other paratroopers. Their task is to search and destroy a group of armed terrorists who have crossed over from Pakistan and are on their way into the Kashmir Valley.

A burst of gunfire suddenly catches them unawares. It comes from behind a ten-foot-high boulder. Raizada shouts out an ear-scalding Hindi swear word and leaps behind a big rock. He looks up and is relieved to find Bisht leaning back against another rock, breathing heavily. With a curt nod in Raizada's direction, gesturing to him to stay put, Bisht slings his rifle on his back and makes a dash for the boulder that is almost twice as tall as he is. Using the momentum from his sprint and the adrenaline in his veins, he grabs the slanting rock and pulls himself up. In seconds he is at the top of the boulder, completely exposed, looking down at three Pakistani terrorists who are crouching behind it and firing at Raizada. They are so engrossed that they don't see him. Bisht puts his gun on multiple fire mode and presses the trigger. He plans to kill all three with a continuous burst. There is a click of the trigger but nothing happens!

Bisht is horrified to discover that his gun has jammed. In the freezing cold, he feels sweat on his forehead. Looking down in desperation, he finds an empty cartridge stuck in the gun breach. Removing it quickly with shaking fingers, he points his gun at the terrorists once again. One of them senses something amiss and is turning his head. As Bisht's dark brown eyes meet the Pakistani's light grey-green ones, they both lift their guns instinctively. Bisht is a fraction of a second faster. He sends a spray of bullets into the stunned

Pakistani's face. The same burst rips across the backs of his two comrades as well. Bisht keeps firing, his arm steady, his face a cold emotionless mask. He stops only after all three have fallen in a pool of blood and he's sure they won't rise again. In their thick *phirans* (long woollen robes), eyes open in shock, weapons fallen by their sides, they look like young boys just out of college. Bisht grimaces and with a sad shrug of his shoulders leaps off the boulder and makes his way to where the hawk-nosed Raizada is waiting for him with respect in his eyes.

* * *

Thirteen years later

'That was a near-death experience,' Colonel Sameer Bisht, SM, who is now serving as Deputy Commander of a Mountain Brigade, tells me in September, 2016.

Sipping a relaxed drink in his tastefully done up sitting room in Dehradun, he says, 'Someone had to die that evening, and it was either them or me.' And this, he says, is the tenet behind every battle a soldier fights. 'You go to fight for *naam*, *namak* and *nishaan*—the honour of your paltan and your country, your loyalty towards the salt you have eaten, and the badge of the Indian Army. But when you are face-to-face with the enemy, you fight for your own life. If you don't kill him, he will kill you. That is the ultimate truth.' The ice cubes clink in his whisky glass as he puts it down, a pensive look on his face.

Bisht comes from a family of soldiers. 'My grandfather was posted to Chaklala, now in Pakistan. He was a jumpmaster, he trained paratroopers. My father was an officer with the Gorkha Rifles.' He opted to be a paratrooper. 'It was my childhood dream to join my father's battalion and here I am,' he smiles. Bisht says what attracted him to the Army was the wonderful brotherhood he saw between his father and his fellow officers, the pride they took in wearing the olive-green uniform and the fact that they were fit, motivated men who were hard-core soldiers and were obviously having fun doing it.

'As kids, we would be taken to parties in the Mess that would carry on till morning, though of course, we were not allowed beyond the TV Room where we would watch ghost movies and devour snacks. There would be picnics on weekends, night rabbit hunts and fishing expeditions, movies in the open-air theatre and sitting under the stars. Life was great and I had decided very early that this was the career I wanted too,' he says.

When he didn't pass the NDA entrance exam, Bisht took admission in Delhi's Hansraj College and cleared the Short Service Commission exams in his third year, eventually joining the Officers Training Academy (OTA) in Chennai. When it came to choosing a branch of the Army to join, he picked the infantry, which made him a foot soldier. Later, he volunteered for the elite Parachute Regiment, which is considered one of the toughest in the Indian Army, and was trained to jump from a plane with a parachute on his back.

'Those of us who choose to join the Army are not looking for a mundane desk job,' he answers. 'It wasn't peculiar to me;

all Army officers look forward to action. After all, that is what we are trained for and that is what we are itching to do.'

Bisht did get to see a lot of action. He served with his unit in Ladakh, in the Siachen glacier which is called the highest battlefield in the world, and also participated in Operation Vijay in 1999 (or what civilians better know as the Kargil War), Operation Rakshak in Kashmir and active operations against rebel groups when on the UN Mission in the Democratic Republic of Congo. He came back a decorated soldier with a Sena Medal (SM) on his shirtfront, making his father, Brigadier B.S. Bisht, also the recipient of a Sena Medal and a Vishisht Seva Medal (VSM), proud of him.

Sharing rations with the bears

Going back to that freezing cold day in the Kashmir Valley, Bisht recounts the operation where he and his men risked their lives to hunt down nearly twenty terrorists who had crossed the LOC with a big stock of weapons and were on their way to creating trouble in Kashmir.

'It was beautiful in September,' he recalls, 'The weather was perfect, the breeze was gentle, the wildflowers had formed a carpet of multicoloured hues under our feet and the birch trees, which we know as Bhojpatra, were shedding their pale, white bark that the men would often peel off and use to write romantic letters home to wives and girlfriends. Sometimes, we would get friendly visits from black bears who would raid our tents and steal our rations but nobody minded since there was enough for man and bear both,' he says. 'It never failed to hit me though just how beautiful Kashmir was and just how ugly the situation.'

Bisht's company was deployed on the Shamshabadi ridgeline that separated the Kupwara sector from the Machal sector in Kashmir. It was on this route that terrorists used to infiltrate India from Pakistan Occupied Kashmir (PoK) and their job was to intercept these missions. Bisht was then a company commander, which meant that he had approximately 100 soldiers under his command. 'We had set up posts along the ridge line at every few kilometres. The men were eager to have an encounter with the terrorists. However, there is a saying in the Army that *"terrorist ke darshan hona bhagwan ke darshan hone ke barabar hai"*. This means that these encounters happen rarely and very few get the opportunity.'

The men were getting along with their duties when one morning the news came that a group of heavily armed terrorists had been spotted high up in the mountains. 'Our commanding officer (CO), Colonel Laove Verma, a tough, no-nonsense, second-generation officer himself, gave orders that I, along with two junior commissioned officers (JCOs) and the High Risk Mission (a team comprising the fittest and best-trained men of the unit), would be airlifted to the area of the operation.'

The men were briefed by their CO. He told them that they would be dropped by helicopter at 16,000 feet in a barren and cold terrain. They would have to be self-sufficient for four days during which they would try to search for and destroy the terrorists. Each man would carry a load of twenty-six kilograms, which would include food, weapons, ammunition and winter clothing. Colonel Verma made it clear to his men that he wanted the terrorists—dead or alive. When their large and scowling CO yelled '*Koi shak?* (Any doubts?)' at his men, there was an equally enthusiastic cry of '*Nahin* (No, Sahib), Sahib,' from the boys. Stifling a smile, Col Verma returned to his tent a satisfied man.

'In war, every soldier prefers to carry ammunition over food since ammunition can make the difference between life and death, whereas it hardly matters if you don't eat for a few days,' says Bisht. When the helicopter came to pick them up, the soldiers were mentally prepared for action. Between the team, they were carrying two medium machine guns, rocket launchers, flamethrowers, light machine guns and a lot of ammunition. 'Medium machine guns are generally very heavy, weighing around sixteen kilograms each but paratroopers use a lighter version without a tripod that weighs approximately twelve kilograms,' explains Bisht. The men were also carrying energy bars, dry fruits and MRE (Meal, Ready-to-Eat) rations containing *parantha*, *sabzi*, *pulao* and *suji ka halwa* that had to be dipped in boiling water for a ready-to-eat meal. Besides this, they also had stoves and kerosene in their backpacks, a necessity at high altitudes.

Hunting demons in the valley

September, 2003
Baraub

Bisht and his men are ferried in batches of six or seven by the chopper and dropped off in the general area where the armed terrorists have been spotted. They look around to find that they are above the tree line with only harsh, rocky, barren mountains all around. 'The terrorists had been spotted near a stream on the other side of the ridge but we were deliberately not dropped there so that we could retain an element of surprise,' Bisht recollects. The men start walking to the top of the ridge, carrying warm inners, woollen balaclava caps and thick socks in their backpacks. It is only when they reach the top that they change out of their sweaty inners and don the cold weather clothing. It is here that they run into the young and handsome, though ill-fated, Lieutenant K.D. Singh and his Ghatak team from the Sikh battalion, also akin to commandos, who have walked the entire distance from Dawar, from where Bisht and his men have been airlifted. They are also carrying a sixteen-kilogram medium machine gun, which is heavier than the one the paratroopers carry, but they have managed to lug it all the way up the ridge. 'We got our maps out and oriented ourselves, trying to work out a plan. Since it would take a while to comb the entire area, and it was getting dark already, we broke into seven teams of six men each, and placed our ambushes about 500 metres from each other all along the ridge line,' Bisht explains. So while K.D. and his men decide to step down into the bowl where there is a stream and trees to take cover, Bisht and his men put up their pup tents and wait and watch through the night. 'It was biting cold, and there was a lot of frost. While four men would sleep in the tent, three would stand guard outside, their teeth chattering in the cold. We would then rotate the duties,' Bisht says.

On 23 September, at first light, the men on the ridge hear gunshots. They simultaneously get a message on their radio set that a Ladakh Scout patrol has run into the terrorists. Armed with only basic INSAS rifles, the Ladakh Scouts are being routed by the heavily armed terrorists who have already shot and injured three of their men.

'This was happening about two kilometres from us in that barren bowl, in the same area where a mountain stream made a fork and there were lots of rocks and boulders for the terrorists to hide behind,' says Bisht. He starts moving his sub teams down. 'There was so much enthusiasm that the men started running,' he recalls. 'In fact, I distinctly remember Raizada encouraging his men shouting *"Tez bhago nahin toh hamare liye ek bhi terrorist nahin bachega!* (Make it quick or there won't be a single terrorist left!)" It was very heartening to see this kind of josh, this fervour, in the men.'

Losing K.D.

Lieutenant K.D. Singh and his team also reach the stream by then. Unfortunately, the handsome and fearless K.D., only twenty-three years old, is shot in the head by a terrorist. He is firing a rocket launcher when a bullet gets him and the young officer falls and dies on the spot. A PARA sub-team replaces the Ghatak platoon and helps in evacuating the officer. 'K.D. was such a brave soldier. He went down fighting and we are so proud of him,' says Bisht, getting sentimental. 'Incidentally, in my current posting in Dehradun, the ground at the brigade headquarter ground is called Lieutenant

K.D. Singh Ground in his memory. Each time I cross it, I think of the comrade we lost that morning in Kashmir. Had he been alive, he would have been thirty-six years old today and most certainly doing very well.'

The firing goes on till the afternoon and at 2 p.m. Bisht can count five bodies. That is when he and Raizada give each other covering fire in turns and reach the boulder behind which the terrorists have taken cover. By the time Bisht climbs up the boulder and shoots the three men holed up behind it, dusk has fallen. The soldiers extricate and place their ambushes for the night. The night is freezing cold and the men are completely exposed to the elements without their tents. To make things worse, it starts raining and then snowing. The soldiers are caught in a nasty blizzard, they are cold and wet, and they haven't eaten since the operation started. 'Food was furthest from our minds,' says Bisht. 'But the cold was lethal. We were chilled to the bone, our teeth were chattering, the dampness had seeped into our shoes and inside our woollen vests. But we had no choice but to hold on.'

The next morning, the search resumes and they find and kill four more terrorists. 'Search and destroy operations (SADO) are the most dangerous,' Bisht explains. 'When you are combing through a terrain, you have no idea who is sitting behind the next boulder and could shoot you in the face before you can react.' This morning, he runs into a terrorist who is shooting at them from behind a cliff. In an attempt to distract him, Bisht engages him in conversation, asking him his name and why he has come to India. The boy, in his early twenties, tells him that he has been told Kashmir is heaven and the

Indians are killing Kashmiris. '*Hum unhe bachane aaye hain. Tu mere raaste se hat ja nahin toh teri biwi bewaa ho jaayegi*, (We are here to save them. Make way for me else your wife would be widowed)' the boy tells Bisht. At that very moment, one of the soldiers flings a grenade at him that sends splinters into his body, making him run out from behind the cliff in shock and pain. Bisht, simply waiting for a chance, shoots him dead.

Another night passes. On the morning of 24 September, after the men have counted a total of fourteen bodies, the artillery officer with them advises them to take cover since he is planning to ask for artillery fire. The soldiers duck behind a cliff and the artillery officer signals his guns. A volley of heavy fire comes to them from the Bofors guns and the other guns lined up seven kilometres away on the highway in a place called Barog. The heavy fire bombards the area for forty-five minutes, causing complete devastation. When the roar of the guns stops, it is obvious that all the terrorists in the area are dead.

The tired and hungry men march in their cold, wet fatigues and move down to makeshift huts, known as dhoks, used by the goat-grazing Bakkarwal nomads. There, they dry their clothes and eat some hot food. It continues to snow for four days and the men keep watch from their huts. On 28 September, news comes that a patrol from the Sikh regiment has encountered two terrorists from the same party. While one has been killed, the other provides information that the last three terrorists are hiding in a dhok further up the ridge. They, too, are killed in an encounter.

When the weather finally turns, the men go up the ridge again and find the bodies of all the fifteen terrorists they have killed. They then walk down to Dawar from where they had been airlifted ten days ago. They are picked up in their unit vehicles and come back to a resounding welcome. Their happiness is dampened only by the loss of Naik Joginder Singh, Bisht's radio operator, who has been shot by a stray bullet. 'We found him lying down and realized he had got shot in the chest. He had died without uttering a word,' says Bisht. The soldiers have made a big recovery of weapons, ammunition and radio sets. It has been one of the biggest terrorist encounters in the history of Kashmir and the Army Chief, General Nirmal Chander Vij himself, pays a visit to congratulate the soldiers.

When it is Subedar Bhim Singh Raizada's turn to shake hands with the Chief, a short man, he looks down from his colossal height.

'Sahib, kya ye aapka pehla operation hain? (Sahib, is this your first operation?)' the soft-spoken General Vij asks Raizada.

The Subedar tries to look polite but breaks into his habitual scowl. 'Sahib, hum ekis saal se yeh hi kar rahe hain, (we've been doing this for 21 years)' he says proudly.

The Chief breaks into a smile and the battalion photographer captures the moment for posterity. That group photograph finds pride of place in the houses of nearly all the men who participated in that operation. It sits on Bisht's study. 'I look at it sometimes and remember that chilly September day when all of us were together on a mission, I think of K.D.

and Joginder who are gone, and then of the others who are standing beside me in the picture in their battered uniforms. My heart fills with love for these men who I know will always stand by me, even facing death. I know it because I would do the same for them,' he says, pouring himself a second drink. 'That's what the Army is all about. That's why I joined.'

The Parachute Regiment—Be a Red Devil

'What manner of men are these who wear the maroon beret?

They are firstly all volunteers, and are then toughened by hard physical training. As a result, they have that infectious optimism and that offensive eagerness which comes from physical well-being. They have jumped from the air and by doing so have conquered fear. Their duty lies in the van of the battle: they are proud of this honour and have never failed in any task. They have the highest standards in all things, whether it be skill in battle or smartness in the execution of all peacetime duties. They have shown themselves to be as tenacious and determined in defence as they are courageous in attack. They are, in fact, men apart—every man an Emperor.'

Field Marshal, First Viscount Montgomery of Alamein

All paratroopers across the world wear a maroon beret and are affectionately called the Red Devils. The role of the paratroopers, who consider themselves tougher than other soldiers, includes being dropped into enemy territory so that

---

they can fight from within and then make their way back to safety. It could also include slithering down from ropes from helicopters that cannot land in enemy territory and being picked up in a similar fashion once they are done with their mission. All paratroopers also wear a wing on their chest.

All Indian paratroopers are volunteers. Some enter the para regiments fresh from recruitment, while others transfer in from regular army units. If you want to be a paratrooper, you will need to volunteer after completing training at the Indian Military Academy (Dehradun) or the Officers Training Academy (Chennai). The chosen few undergo a tough probation and if they are confirmed, they turn into airborne soldiers who possess the power to jump from a moving aircraft with parachutes on their backs.

3

'She was stuck thirty feet underground in a narrow borewell.'

Lieutenant Colonel Rajesh Unnikrishnan of an independent Parachute Field Company, part of the Army's Corps of Engineers, remembers the dark night when he and his men went thirty feet under the ground to rescue a baby who had fallen into an abandoned borewell.

26 March, 2008, Tehra village
Twenty kilometres away from Agra

The night is dark and hushed. If you listen carefully, you can hear laboured breathing and the sound of mud being shovelled. About thirty feet under the ground, four men in Army fatigues are working hard by the light of the lamps fitted to their helmets. Three of them stand by, waiting for shovels full of wet mud to be thrown back at them. They are packing the mud into a bucket hanging from a rope, and then giving the rope a tug to alert people at ground level to pull it out. Captain Rajesh Unnikrishnan of the independent Parachute Field Company, part of the Army's Corps of Engineers, is inside a dark tunnel, four feet in diameter. If he wants to stand up, he can't. Fighting the muscle ache that has set in from being on his haunches for hours, Rajesh uses a shovel to dig deeper. All of a sudden, a baby's frightened cry pierces the silence. He stiffens for a moment and then he grits his teeth and starts shovelling mud frantically. It has been nearly thirty-six hours since the little girl has been trapped. He has to save her—come what may!

* * *

25 March, 2008
Agra

Twenty-seven-year-old Captain Rajesh Unnikrishnan is sitting in his office when the phone rings. It is his Officer Commanding, Lieutenant Colonel Rajeev Kaul, who tells him that Vandana, a two-year-old girl, has fallen into an abandoned borewell in Tehra, a village twenty kilometres away from Agra. Rajesh is asked to immediately put together a team of three soldiers and go assess the situation. He picks the best men he has and drives forty-five minutes to the village. By the time the soldiers reach Tehra, it is 9 p.m. and darkness has fallen. By the light of halogen lamps, they see a crowd of around forty people sitting around a borehole. The silence of the night is punctuated by the heart-wrenching cries of the frightened baby who has fallen down the dark hole.

'When I peered into the hole which was only six inches in diameter, as wide as the length of a geometry box scale, I saw nothing. But the child was down somewhere because I could hear her crying,' recounts the gentle and unassuming Rajesh (now a Lieutenant Colonel) nearly eight years later. 'Vandana's parents were trying to comfort her and each time they spoke to her, she would answer back so we were reassured to know that she was fine.'

Using a flashlight, Rajesh can make out the child's head. She seems to be stuck vertically in the narrow pit, her thin body pressing against the mud walls. 'Her parents told me that she had been running after some older children when she stepped into the hole. Being a very thin child, she just slipped right into it,' he says. By then, a doctor has also reached the location and a tube connected to an oxygen cylinder has been pushed down the hole so that Vandana does not suffocate. The rescue mission is in full swing.

A rope is lowered into the hole and when it touches the child, they pull it out and measure just how deep she has fallen—twenty-seven feet. 'It was a miracle that she had not fallen deeper. In Uttar Pradesh, the water table is quite low and borewells often go down to 150 feet but she had obviously, and thankfully, gotten stuck in between,' explains Rajesh.

The rescue

It is decided to dig a parallel pit, seven feet from the borewell hole, connect the two shafts horizontally and pull the child out. At 11.30 p.m., the digging starts. A giant excavator with a big bucket is put to work. 'The child had stopped crying by then. We assumed that she had either become unconscious due to fatigue or had gone to sleep,' Rajesh says. A pit twelve feet in diameter is being dug by the machine, throwing out mountains of mud as it whirs into action. Work progresses fast but around 4 a.m., when they reach a depth of fifteen feet, the men realize that the arm of the excavator will not go any deeper—the rest of the digging will have to be done manually. The four men get into the pit and are joined by enthusiastic villagers who come with their own spades and trowels. 'Some of them were men who dug wells professionally and they were very quick and efficient,' remembers Rajesh.

By then, twenty-five more soldiers have been sent to assist with the rescue and they take turns at digging the pit. The men work through the night, stopping only for water breaks. By 11 a.m., the men have reached a depth of twenty-seven feet, the depth at which Vandana has fallen. 'We decided to dig another five feet to ensure that the horizontal tunnel we planned to dig would not open on top of the child. There was a risk that the mud would suffocate her,' says Rajesh. Meanwhile, Vandana asks her parents for milk and it is passed down in a small cup with a handle tied to a rope. 'I'm not sure if she drank it or it got spilt along the way,' says Rajesh. 'Some glucose biscuits were also sent to her the same way.'

By 1 p.m., the men manage to go down thirty feet and decide to connect the two pits. The original team of four takes over this sensitive operation and using smaller spades and trowels, they start digging a horizontal connecting tunnel. The men have been working almost non-stop, they are hungry and tired but their spirits are high. From time to time, they can hear the frightened baby crying and that keeps them going.

'It was very tiring work. The tunnel was just about four feet in diameter and it was claustrophobic to work in such a confined space. One person would sit on his haunches and dig, while the other would collect the mud and send it up. Work progressed painfully slow. Very frankly, the child's pitiful cries were our biggest motivation. She was fighting to stay alive,' admits Rajesh.

Strangely enough, when the men had started digging the parallel pit, it had been kept at a distance of seven feet from the borehole but when they start working on the connecting tunnel, it seems to have gone further away. 'We realized that the distance separating the two pits was now more than fourteen feet because during our manual digging in the dark, the direction of the rescue pit had changed,' Rajesh explains. A fourteen-foot-long horizontal tunnel now needs to be dug to connect the two holes. It is dangerous work since the men are thirty feet underground and the tunnel has no reinforcements at the top.

This tunnel is just four feet wide and Rajesh is six feet inside and squatting on his thighs, digging gently, when the roof collapses as feared and he is buried under the mud. His men panic a little but they reach out in the loose, wet mud and find his foot. He is pulled out in time. It is a near escape but after he has cleaned the mud out of his eyes and ears and coughed up whatever is stuck in his mouth, it makes Rajesh more determined than ever to save the child.

Their Officer Commanding, who is monitoring the operation from the ground, gets worried when he is told that mud is caving in from the roof of the tunnel. Since his prime concern is the safety of his men, he orders the team to use barrels to ensure the tunnel does not collapse on them, or he will make them abort the operation. A few 200-litre barrels are sent down into the pit. The rescue team tries to dig by crawling through them but it is taking a lot of time. 'The four of us had a quick conversation and at 8 p.m. we decided we would not use the barrels. We were so determined to save the girl that we decided we would prefer to die there rather than call off the rescue. We didn't send those barrels up though. We did not want the OC to know we were not using them,' Rajesh discloses.

Using handheld search lights and helmets with lights for illumination, the men keep digging. 'The tunnel got so narrow that we had to lie on our stomachs to dig further. We started tying ourselves to each other with ropes so that we could be pulled out if it collapsed again,' recounts Rajesh.

As the men start getting closer to the borewell hole, they use an instrument called an electronic stethoscope. Normally used in bomb disposal operations to locate hidden ticking explosive devices, it starts beeping if it detects a regular ticking sound. They hope that it will catch the child's heartbeat. When they are thirteen feet inside the tunnel, the electronic stethoscope suddenly starts emitting a distinct sound. A smile of pleasure runs across each of the mud-streaked faces of the four men—they are close to the child.

They then speak to the team outside on their handset. It is decided that a Motorola handset should be lowered into the borewell with the beep mode on. 'We were hoping that the stethoscope would catch the sound and point us in the exact direction of the child. The experiment worked perfectly though it also scared the child who had no idea what the noise was,' says Rajesh.

He is digging gently when he hits open space. Realizing that he has reached the borewell shaft, he pushes his hands up the hole. 'I could touch the girl's legs. I tried to pull her out but she wouldn't move.' Feeling around in the dark, Rajesh realizes that some roots have got entangled with the girl's leg just above the knee. He pulls at them till they break away. Then, very gently, he reaches out for the child and pulls her down. She slides into his arms easily, crying in fear. Holding her close, Rajesh assures her that she is safe. He climbs up the ladder in the pit and then wrapping her in a blanket that has been thrown down to him, he sends her up with another officer. The time is 9.40 p.m. on 26 March.

By the time Rajesh pulls himself out of the thirty-foot pit, Vandana's parents have taken her to SN Medical College in Agra. The Captain and his men return to their unit, hungry and tired. They haven't slept for two days and two nights. Driving back, their tired, dirty faces relax, even though they can still taste the salty borewell mud that seems to have got stuck not just under their hair, their clothes and their nails but also deep inside their throats and the gaps between their teeth.

As the days pass, Rajesh watches Vandana's progress through television reports, rushing to his room to switch on the TV whenever he has time. Two months later, he decides to visit the girl he helped rescue. 'When I reached the village and looked for their house, I was told that Vandana's parents had moved away with her. I was never able to meet her again,' he says with a gentle smile. The names of the rescue team are recommended for awards but only two of the soldiers get commendations from the Army Chief. Rajesh did not get an award but when you mention this to him, he looks surprised.

'Vandana survived. That was the biggest award I could have got.' A smile lights up his face.

An unfortunate episode

A little after the Vandana rescue, Captain Rajesh Unnikrishnan got another SOS call. In another village near Agra, a small child had got stuck in another borewell hole. The same team was sent again to lead the rescue effort. This time it was a little boy who had slipped nearly seventy-six feet into a hole that was eight inches in diameter. 'The boy's parents came to me; they had heard about the earlier rescue and were very hopeful that we would be able to save their child too,' recounts Rajesh.

The team got down to work immediately. The same technique of digging a parallel pit was used this time as well. 'It was a gruelling 109-hour operation,' says Rajesh. 'We decided that we would not move out of the pit till we got the child'. The men eventually managed to reach the child. 'When I pulled the boy out, I could smell the decomposition. His ribs had pierced his heart and he was dead.' Rajesh passed the child's body up the pit to his waiting parents. For a long time he did not emerge himself—he just sat there crying. Ironically, he was awarded a commendation from the Chief of Army Staff for his brave effort. 'I don't even feel like putting it on my uniform,' he says quietly. 'It only reminds me that we could not save that child.' However, he remembers the life he *had* saved sometimes, and that makes it hurt less.

Be an engineer with the Corps of Engineers

You can be an engineer and an Army officer at the same time. The Army has direct entry schemes for young people who would like to join the Corps of Engineers. If you score more than 70 per cent in the physics, chemistry and mathematics (PCML) group of subjects in the twelfth standard examinations and you appear on the Army's merit list, you are invited to an interview and physicals directly. The Army then enables you to complete your engineering studies from its colleges while paying you a stipend. You are then given a degree from the Indira Gandhi National Open University (IGNOU).

You can also opt to join the Corps of Engineers after completing postgraduate studies or post training at the IMA or the OTA. Selected officers undergo a three-year engineering degree at the beautiful College of Military Engineering in Pune and get their degree from IGNOU.

If you are an engineering graduate you can join the Army as an engineer by writing the Combined Defence Services examination (CDS) and undergoing training at the IMA. The

Indian Army Corps of Engineers consists of three groups of combat engineers—the Madras Sappers, the Bengal Sappers and the Bombay Sappers. Each group consists of a number of engineer regiments. The job of combat engineer regiments in war is to support the fighting soldiers by constructing bridges and helipads, detecting and removing mines laid out by the enemy. They also lay minefields for the enemy and demolish enemy bridges if required.

They are also called sappers and miners. Sapping is the process of digging trenches, which could either be covered or open and laid out in a zig-zag fashion to help attacking soldiers reach the enemy undetected. Corps of Engineers officers also serve in major engineering organizations like the Military Engineering Service (MES), that takes on major building maintenance and construction for all three forces—Army, Navy and Air Force and the Border Roads Organization (BRO), that has been involved in constructing national highways, bridges, airfields and so on. The Engineers have had a major role to play in building schools, hospitals, living accommodation for serving soldiers and in connecting remote areas like Ladakh, Spiti, Arunachal to the rest of civilization. You can get to do any or all of this by joining the Army as an engineer.

4

'We aimed for zero collateral damage.'

Colonel S.S. Shekhawat, Special Forces; the most highly decorated serving officer of the Indian Army and the leader of the Loktak Lake Operation, talks about some of the adventures he has had.

8 September 2008, 1 a.m.
Loktak Lake, Manipur

It's a dark night. The thirty-foot-deep Loktak Lake stretches out like an unending ocean, disturbed only by the soft splash of oars moving through the water. Three narrow canoes, eight feet long, are making their way over its cold depths, each seating armed soldiers in diving gear. In his black neoprene wetsuit, a TAR-21 rifle slung across his back, Lieutenant Colonel Saurabh Singh Shekhawat of the PARA (Special Forces) blends in completely with the night. Even if he stretches out his finely muscled arm in front of his face, he cannot see it. This fills him with relief—it means the enemy can't see him either. Surprise is the single biggest factor that will ensure his twelve men and he come back alive from the suicidal mission they are on. Courage stamped across his handsome face, Shekhawat tells himself he will not let his men down. Then, lowering his head, he starts rowing again.

* * *

October, 2016
Delhi

How many people have the opportunity to drink a cup of coffee brewed by the most highly decorated serving officer in the Indian Army? A man who is a three-time gallantry award winner, three-time Everest summiteer, free faller, horseman, marathoner, who has saved lives, risked his own many times and taken some too. Not many, I'm sure, have had that coffee. But I did. On a balmy October morning in the year 2016, I drive down to the Institute for Defence Services and Analyses, New Delhi to interview the dashing now Colonel Saurabh Singh Shekhawat, Kirti Chakra (KC), Shaurya Chakra (SC), Sena Medal (SM), Vishist Seva Medal (VSM). He gallantly offers to make me some coffee and I immediately agree. He soon hands me a steaming hot mug, and I settle down on his office sofa to hear the adventures of a lifetime.

'It was a pitch-dark, moonless night,' Colonel Shekhawat tells me, talking about the Loktak Lake Operation, as I wait for my coffee to cool a bit. 'And that is exactly why it was chosen for the strike.' The team of twelve Special Forces men, the toughest soldiers in the Indian Army—free fallers, swimmers, weapons and unarmed combat experts, especially trained for the most dangerous missions—have been rowing on the lake for close to three-and-a-half hours. They have covered nearly seven kilometres. Their task is to destroy a militant camp on an island on Loktak Lake.

Navigating around the floating biomass that has ten-foot-tall grass growing on it is not easy even in the daylight but they are doing it in the night—in zero visibility. They have a guide with them, a man whose brother was kidnapped by the militants but he escaped and came back home. The militants have threatened to kill him, which is why he is leading the soldiers to their hideout. When the guide whispers that they are nearly there, Shekhawat picks up his night-vision binoculars and climbs on to the platform fixed on the canoe to enable the men to see above the ten-foot-tall grass all around.

The island is right in front of him. The guide identifies the three huts where the militants are holed up. A light burns in one of them and he can see a sentry with a gun on the roof. Below there are two more armed men. All around are huts of the locals. Shekhawat has been told that innocent people must not be harmed. 'Zero collateral damage is a very tough condition in any operation,' he says. 'We are always told that a terrorist can make his escape but a civilian should not be harmed.' That is the reason why the Special Forces team has been practising and planning the attack for nearly a month. They have carried out thirty rehearsals to ensure that nothing goes wrong at the last moment.

In freezing water

The initial plan is that the Special Forces team will swim to the island, which is seven kilometres from the shore. For a week during training, they swim long distances in the ice-cold water. 'Since it is a top-secret operation, we would start training after the villages around had gone to sleep, around 11 p.m., and end by 3 a.m., just before the fishermen wake up for the morning catch. It would all be done in the dark,' explains Shekhawat. However, he soon realizes that they are not able to cover a distance of more than five kilometres, in spite of swimming for seven hours at a time. 'Moreover, the water was at a temperature of two to five degrees centigrade and even in our wetsuits, supposedly cold resistant, we would get chilled to the bone,' he says. In one week of practice, each of the men has lost about three kilograms, two of them have to be admitted to the Intensive Care Unit, severely ill from their nightly excursions in the cold water. Eventually, Shekhawat aborts this plan because he realizes it won't work.

They decide that they will reach the island like local fishermen—using canoes. 'What we didn't know then was that rowing a canoe is like riding a bicycle—till you learn how to do it right, you just keep falling off,' he grimaces. For twenty days, again with the cover of night, the men practise diligently and slowly, they become experts. 'We could also row fast and noiselessly and manoeuvre our boats around the tricky land masses floating on the lake. We also ensured that our practice was a complete secret from all local people. Since the lake was so huge, we picked an area that was completely deserted,' explains Shekhawat.

Meanwhile, the militant group has been running amok, carrying out one heinous act after another. They have attacked the residence of the chief minister of Manipur, attacked the Parliament while it is in session and have started abducting children as child soldiers and extorting large sums from the locals. No one has been able to stop them so far and the final straw is when on 6 September, the group attacks a Gorkha Rifles unit. Having exercised restraint so far due to the possibility of collateral damage, the Army top brass give Shekhawat and his men orders to destroy the militant camp.

The strike

It is 2 a.m. when the boats reach the island. Shekhawat gets on the makeshift platform and trains his binoculars at the huts his source has pointed out. He makes a move, and being a big man, upsets the balance of the canoe. It turns over, toppling all six soldiers, including Shekhawat, into the freezing water; the soldiers grimace about the clumsiness of their leader but make no noise. They straighten the canoe and clamber back in, taking care not to topple it again.

Shekhawat feels a gust of cold air at the back of his wet head. He freezes and orders the men to stop rowing. 'The gust I felt meant that the wind was blowing in the direction of the island and the noise of our oars would be heard by their sentry. I did not want to take that risk,' he says. The canoe is turned around and the men enter the floating biomass and navigate their way to the other side of the island. It takes them an hour and a half of strenuous rowing to get close again. This time, they find a big piece of floating biomass over which they pull their canoes so that they become steady. All twelve soldiers climb on top of the platforms and look through their night-vision binoculars. The island has a total of thirteen huts of which three belong to the militants and the rest to the fishermen.

The responsibility of ensuring that no innocent people are hurt in the fight weighs heavily on Shekhawat's mind and he individually checks with each man about what he is seeing. He is also bogged down by the fact that he has not allowed his team to wear bulletproof vests because these would have made them sink in the water. They are wearing life jackets, which will help them float if they fall into the lake but they will also become easy targets for the enemy. 'Our intelligence network had informed us that the militants had an impressive array of weapons at their disposal. These included a 7.62 RPD machine gun, an M79 grenade launcher (lethod), M16 and AK-47 assault rifles and shoulder-fired rocket-propelled grenades (RPGs) with the power to destroy tanks,' reminisces Shekhawat. He watches closely and when the guard leaves the machan at 3 a.m., he gives his men orders to open fire.

Shoot to kill

'Six of us stood shoulder-to-shoulder on the wooden platform in each boat, our weapons trained at the three militant huts. I told them to open fire.' All hell then breaks loose. The men fire from their assault rifles, machine guns, multi-grenade launchers. The terrorist sentry and perimeter patrol fire back at Shekhawat and his men but fall to the fusillade of bullets sent by Shekhawat's machine gunner. The fire lasts exactly four minutes and causes complete devastation. After they are satisfied that the camp has been neutralized, the soldiers jump into the water and swim to the island. They find that except for one lady with an M16 gun, who has sustained a bullet injury, the terrorists have all been killed. After giving her a dexamethasone injection to treat shock and ensure functioning of her vital organs, the lady is sent to a hospital and she survives.

The high point of the operation is that not one civilian is injured in the exchange of fire and there is not a scratch on any of Shekhawat's boys. The Special Forces men row their canoes back to camp, weary but satisfied. They come back to a piping hot glass of tea. 'It was the best chai of my life,' says Colonel Shekhawat. He is later awarded the Kirti Chakra, the second highest peacetime gallantry award of the Indian Army.

Losing a friend on the Everest and other mountaineering memories

His coffee finished, Colonel Shekhawat leans back in his chair and recounts a scary adventure he had in 2004 while climbing Mount Nun, the highest peak in the Himalayas within the Indian side of the LOC. 'I was the first one climbing while also fixing ropes for the other men to follow me up the seventy-degree slope. There was an overhang in front of me that I was not being able to reach because I was tied to the person behind me. Since it looked fairly easy, I made a cardinal mistake. I unhooked myself from the other climbers and stepped on a ledge to fix my ice axe. All of a sudden, the ice block broke and I fell. Since we were on a traverse, there was a row of my boys standing below. They saw me falling and instead of jumping aside to save themselves, two of them pounced on me and held on tightly.'

With the sheer force of his fall, Shekhawat took both down with himself. Since they were tied to two others, all five fell down the steep incline and were plummeting down the icy mountain at top speed. Luckily, Shekhawat and another man managed to anchor their ice axes in the ice and all five came to a halt just before a sheer drop of 800 feet. They escaped death, though their clothes were torn and they were bleeding and scratched all over. 'That incident taught me how, in the Army, your men will never leave your side even if death is staring them in the face,' says an emotional Shekhawat.

A year later, he got a chance to do the same on an Everest summit. 'I've climbed Everest thrice,' he says humbly. 'I still remember the dates of reaching the summit: on 23 May 2001, 22 May 2003 and 2 June, 2005.' One of his most challenging ascents, he says, was in 2005 when an Army team and an Air Force team were both attempting the summit at the same time. 'There was a short window of good weather lasting two days and the Air Force team decided to go for it. They reached the summit but on the way back, the weather worsened and in low visibility and high winds, one of their members, Squadron

Leader Chaitanya, and his Sherpa guide were separated from the main team.

Shekhawat says he received a message from the Air Force team leader requesting help to trace the officer. 'The weather had become really bad, the wind was blowing at 100 kilometres per hour when Sherpa Sardar and I tried to move up. Despite our best efforts, we could climb only twenty metres in forty minutes,' he remembers. The weather became so threatening that the two experienced mountaineers just couldn't go ahead. Sherpa Sardar held his hand and pulled him saying, 'Give up, Sahib, there is no chance we can reach the IAF team. If we stay here any longer, we will not be able to get back either.'

Shekhawat says his legs froze. 'In the forces, we are morally bound to help people, and the life of a fellow officer was involved. I was so upset that we could not go on but finally, I had to listen to Sherpa Sardar.' The two returned to their camp in near-zero visibility, battling their way through a blizzard. On his radio set, a very frustrated and upset Shekhawat heard the last communication Chaitanya had with his team leader. He was saying, 'Sir, I am feeling very cold.' 'We later found out that Chaitanya was unable to move because of the cold and fatigue. His Sherpa tried to convince him to climb down but finally left him to save his own life. Chaitanya, in his hypoxiated mind, where an oxygen-deprived brain begins to get confused and disoriented, probably tried moving down and fell. We never found him—just one abandoned crampon. We lost Chaitanya on the intervening night of 29 May–30 May,' he says softly.

This tragic incident played on Shekhawat's mind when he took the Army's women's team on the summit soon after they lost Chaitanya. On 2 June, the team reached the Everest summit but joy was missing from that achievement. On the return journey, one of the lady officers developed extreme fatigue and hypoxia, a condition that strikes mountaineers at heights above 8000 metres—most likely the same thing that had happened to Chaitanya. 'Your brain gives commands but your body refuses to follow them,' Shekhawat explains. 'Our team was very strong but even then it took a lot of effort and mental strength for the boys and Sherpas to assist her down. Every four hours, I would give her a dexamethasone injection to kick-start her vital organs. It took us twenty-six hours to bring her back to the camp but we did it,' he says. 'That was a bigger achievement than the actual summit.'

A skydiving misadventure

Shekhawat recounts a skydiving experience, this one from when he was commanding his unit in the year 2013 in Jorhat 'We Indians jump with rucksacks tied to our backs; they hang over behind our legs making us walk like penguins, but they don't create any disturbance during skydiving,' he says. 'Then I saw Americans jumping. They had the rucksacks on their fronts so I decided I would try the same.' During a routine free fall in February 2013, he boldly tied his rucksack to his front and jumped out of the plane with his buddy (from buddies in arms—one supports the other and

covers him in combat situations) Pramod Shinde jumping after him.

'During skydiving training, we are taught to jump out facing the earth. But the moment I jumped out of the plane, I turned and was sky facing because my rucksack in front played some aerodynamic trick.' When he tried to turn around, he got caught in air currents and started spinning at full speed. 'The spin is so bad that it can make you vomit in seconds,' he says. Shekhawat quickly pulled out his parachute. Unfortunately, it got caught between his legs because his body was spinning. 'In such cases the general procedure is that you cut it away and open your reserve parachute but again, I made a cardinal mistake—I decided I would unravel my parachute from between my legs and not open my reserve, which I was supposed to as per the practice. Being an experienced free faller, Shekhawat managed to straighten out his parachute at 900 feet and landed safely.

Meanwhile, Shinde had seen Shekhawat struggling to open his parachute. Being an accomplished skydiver, he could reach a person falling ahead of him, hold him and help him correct his position. Shinde did not open his own parachute and started coming towards Shekhawat to help him out. Shekhawat sorted out his tangled parachute but Shinde did not realize that he had gone below 750 feet without opening his own parachute. His emergency parachute automatically opened even as Shinde pulled open his main parachute. The two parachutes could have tangled causing a serious emergency but being an expert, Shinde could cut away his main parachute and landed with his reserve. 'He put his life on line for me that day,' says an overwhelmed Shekhawat.

A man who got a bullet in his head and other bravehearts

Ask Shekhawat about the motivation behind his countless medals and what makes him put his life in danger time and again and he smiles and says, 'I like to challenge myself; overcoming difficult situations gives me a lot of personal satisfaction. The Army has been very kind to me but I don't do it for awards.'

Shekhawat gives a lot of credit to the Special Forces training for making him who he is. 'I look at people like Major Deependra Singh Sengar, SM, a senior of mine, who walks around with six bullets in his body; or Major Ashish Sonal, VRC, who got a bullet in his head in Sri Lanka and started writing books; or Colonel Ivan Joseph Crasto, KC, our former CO, who did that famous Timber Trail chair car rescue and I feel humbled. I see the same fire in many of our youngsters and I am sure they are going to do great things ahead. All of us in the Special Forces have some extra frequency in our brain. That is what makes us test ourselves again and again,' he says with a smile.

Requesting him for a picture, for my personal album, that he smilingly agrees to, I say goodbye to the Indian Army's most highly decorated officer. He is preparing for some bareback horse riding and show jumping when we part and says he is waiting to see what life throws at him next.

Read more about the Special Forces on page 178.

In Extremis

How do they get their thrills?

They jump out of planes, fly in a wingsuit, climb the Everest, go on ski expeditions to the South Pole. And yes, this includes lady officers too!

5

'Jumping out of a plane makes me feel alive!'

Lieutenant Colonel Satyendra Verma (Retd.), from the Corps of Signals, one of the Army's most famous skydivers, talks about the thrill he gets from jumping off planes and buildings.

16 December 2012
10,000 feet above the Arabian Sea
Near Mumbai

For most of Mumbai, it is just another December afternoon. For Lieutenant Colonel Satyendra Verma, sitting in the Indian Army's Dhruv helicopter, cruising 10,000 feet above the Arabian Sea, it is a lot more special. Zipped up in his black and orange wingsuit, a helmet clamped firmly over his head, he looks like a superhero on a mission. Peering out of the open chopper door, Verma looks at the dull, blue stretch of the Arabian Sea curving into the Mumbai shoreline below.

As always, he mentally rehearses the emergency procedures to be undertaken just in case things go wrong and then, reaching out, he activates the smoke flares attached to his boots. Usually, they take a few seconds to light up and he is out of the plane before that happens but today they seem to work in fast forward. A swirl of thick orange smoke fills up the chopper almost immediately, creating a scare. 'It's me,' Verma hastily calls out to the alarmed pilot. 'I'm just leaving.' With a cheerful thumbs up, he spreads his wings and dives down.

* * *

October, 2016
Delhi

Thanks to a cancelled Uber ride and delay in finding another one due to bad internet connectivity in the Air Force Station, Palam (where I live), I am nearly half an hour late for my 1 p.m. Connaught Place appointment with the daredevil skydiver. Since he is leaving for the World Wingsuit Flying Championship in Skydive City, Zephyrhills, United States, the next day and really rushed, he offers to meet me halfway.

And that's how—over a baked fish and steamed rice lunch in a Malcha Marg restaurant that day—I meet my old classmate Satyendra Verma, who used to ride a battered black bicycle to St John's College, Agra, with his hair falling on his forehead twenty-seven years back, and is now one of India's most famous skydivers, though with a shorter haircut. This time, we don't laugh over class gossip but have a serious conversation about those death-defying flights he has made an integral part of his life and is usually too embarrassed to talk about.

'That morning of the wingsuit flight, I knew Mahim Bay looked calm and placid, but it hid some sharp rocks,' he tells me, giving an insight into what goes on in his mind when he is about to jump from those dizzy heights. The rocks, he says, were just one of his worries. 'When you jump out of a plane on a wingsuit, you fly at 200 kilometres per hour, which is more than twice most normal cars' top speed. There is a risk of going into a deadly spin from which it can be extremely difficult to recover.' It needs nerves of steel to jump when you know all this, but it needs luck too. And that's why, Satyendra says, even after all the jumps he has done, he can never be sure how the next will go till it's actually done. That morning it went flawlessly.

Nearly 10,000 feet above the sea with just the wind beneath him, he felt the powerful tug of gravity but the air pockets of his wings filled up quickly and his wingsuit lifted him into horizontal flight. He steered himself towards Shivaji Park and gliding like a giant flying squirrel for two kilometres, took less than a minute to reach the 'Know your Army' mela which was his place of drop. At 4,000 feet over the ground, he opened his parachute. 'That was the first time I relaxed that day. A sense of peace finally enveloped me. I had done the rest of it thousands of times,' he says, forking a piece of fish into his mouth and chewing on it thoughtfully.

* * *

Meanwhile, in the commentator's room at Shivaji Park, the smoke trail had been spotted a while ago and the flight announced to the excited crowd. People had trained their eyes and binoculars on the smoke ribbon in the sky that had magically transformed into a man in a bat suit, who was now hovering above them. To the sound of applause and excited chattering, Satyendra glided to the ground, making a perfect landing on his feet. He was greeted by shrieking children and crowds chanting '*Bharat Mata ki Jai!*' Curious kids who wanted to know if he was a man or a plane, where his engine was, where his wings were, if he was Batman or Superman or what, immediately mobbed him for handshakes. 'It was a very special moment,' he recollects, smiling that old familiar smile.

Bitten by the adventure bug

Satyendra joined the Corps of Signals in 1991 after he graduated from the IMA. He says he was exposed to the olive-green uniform early since his father was a physical training instructor in the Army. The Army attracted him because as a young boy he could see how it nurtured a sense of sportsmanship and adventure. 'During my graduation studies, I would often ask myself if I would get these opportunities for adventure in other careers. I always reached the conclusion that I wouldn't.'

The Army was the only organization he knew of that promoted adventure as a way of life. It took him some time though to figure out the connection between adventure sports and being a soldier but he says he understands it well now.

'They add tranquillity and fearlessness to a person's character which could be crucial at the moment you come face-to-face with the enemy in battle,' he explains.

In his journey as an adventurer, Satyendra says he learnt the importance of staying calm in life-threatening situations. He shares an incident to illustrate this.

Airborne, on a glider he didn't know how to fly

Dehradun, 1993

Captain Satyendra Verma is sitting in a single-seater microlight aircraft that, bizarre as it sounds, is essentially a hang-glider with a Yezdi motorcycle engine strapped to its wheels. Being a single-seater, it cannot carry an instructor so Satyendra has to be fully confident about handling it on the ground before he takes off on his first flight. He is not taking any chances and patiently does one taxi run after another under the eagle eye of his instructor. For many hours, he has been ground flying. It's a bit of a paradox, and means he is starting the engine and speeding up the microlight, bringing it rushing down the airstrip and then stopping it just before it can take off. It is getting extremely monotonous but he knows that it is the only way to learn.

This time, he starts the engine and begins to taxi on the airstrip as fast as he has been instructed to do. The plane rumbles with the familiar sound of the Yezdi engine growling its displeasure at being switched from a motorcycle to a strange aircraft. At the end of the airstrip, Satyendra presses the accelerator just a fraction harder than required at the same time as a gust of wind builds up. Before he realizes what has happened, the confused young Captain finds himself fifty feet up in the air, looking down at his furious instructor.

Satyendra is in an aircraft he has no idea how to fly and as soon as the horror of the situation dawns upon him, he freezes. But then he quickly tells himself that panicking is not an option. He has seen others crashing in similar situations because they panicked. He reassures himself that this is just a hang-glider with an engine and he has flown plenty of hang-gliders before. Calming down, he switches off the engine and then pulling the wings in, tries to descend. The furious face of his instructor dances in front of his eyes and he ensures that he does not make any jerky movements that might crash the plane. He watches the wind take over and push the aircraft beyond the runway. Letting it go free, Satyendra lands it on a piece of rough unploughed land. As the plane taxies to a halt, he closes his eyes in relief. He opens them only when he hears the breathless voice of his instructor who has come running to check on his errant pupil. Teacher glares at student for a while and then they both break into smiles of relief.

Diving from a flying plane

Twenty-three years have passed since that windy Dehradun morning but Satyendra says he still reminds himself of this incident each time he is training for a new sport or using new equipment. 'I tell myself that anything can go wrong on the very first day and if it does, staying calm is the only thing that can save my life.'

He says he remembered this when he went skydiving for the first time, on a freak paragliding flight that lasted more than an hour and the time he jumped off the Kuala Lumpur tower. That was the day when Satyendra, then a skydiver and BASE jumper with the Army Adventure Wing, took the elevator up the Kuala Lumpur tower in Malaysia, stood at the edge, took a cursory look at the cars plying 920 feet below and flung himself off with an unopened parachute strapped to his back. He was practising BASE jumping, a sport where a person jumps from stationary objects like bridges, antennae, spans (bridges) or earth (BASE) instead of an aircraft.

It can't be easy to jump out of a moving plane I ask him. Doesn't his brain tell him to go back in and sit down?

'It does,' he admits but adds that it is this very battle between body and mind that makes skydiving so fascinating. 'The adrenaline is coursing through your veins because all your natural instincts are telling you it is crazy to jump. You just ignore everything that your body tells you, calm your mind by thinking about the confidence you have in your training, the packed parachute and what is expected ahead and simply jump. It makes me feel alive and in control of my senses and this is very important for me,' he says.

The first skydive

When I knew him in college, Satyendra did want to join the Army. I remember him and a few other skinny Army buff classmates swaggering around in their National Cadet Corps (NCC) uniforms; and also a letter that came in the post one day, when I had left Agra to study journalism in Delhi, saying he had got through. Soon after that, we lost touch. So when did he get bitten by the skydiving bug? 'Initially, I just wanted to be an Army officer,' he says, explaining that it probably bit him when he attended a training camp organized by the Army Adventure Wing, a special department in the Army that promotes adventure sports. 'I did my first jump at twenty-three. It was from a single-engine, fixed-wing Beaver aircraft normally used by the Ministry of Agriculture for cloud seeding.' He confesses that he had no idea then that a few years later, he would be skydiving so well that he would rise to becoming an instructor and get posted to the Army Adventure Wing. 'There I was given the opportunity to raise an Army sports skydiving team. That was an important milestone in my life. I got to interact with so many enthusiastic young men who had volunteered to be part of the team and we went on to represent the country in various international competitions.'

Over the years, he went on to BASE jumping and wingsuit flying. Though he opted for premature retirement from the Army, he holds the distinction of being one of its most accomplished skydivers with 2,000 skydives, fifty-three base jumps and 300-plus wingsuit flights to his credit.

Due to the lower altitudes of the jumps, which provides very little time to open a parachute, BASE jumping is considered much more dangerous than skydiving from a plane. When I ask him about this, he says it is prohibited in many places due to its extreme nature and the fact that jumping off buildings, bridges and other places within cities is almost always against the law. People who have tried BASE jumps from the Eiffel Tower or St Louis Arch have been arrested. I want to know more about the famous BASE jump he did from the 450-foot deck of the 771-foot Pitampura TV Tower in New Delhi in the year 2010. He tells me the complete story that had been splashed all over the media and I had read earlier only in bits and pieces.

October 2010, Delhi

It is a breezy October morning and dawn is just breaking. Lieutenant Colonel Satyendra Verma is ready for his first BASE jump in India. Since this is the first time a BASE jump is being tried by the Army, there is naturally a lot of excitement, apprehension and media interest around it. Most television channels and newspapers have stationed correspondents at the jump venue. Verma has packed his parachute with the help of his friend, Wing Commander Kamal Singh Oberh, a famous man himself because he is the first Indian to skydive over both the Arctic and Antarctica.

Driving down to Pitampura, the two of them take the creaky, old pigeon-infested lift up the tower and climb up a rickety metal ladder to a height that can easily give lesser mortals heart attacks. They stand on the narrow metal platform fixed at the top. While Verma stands facing the sharp 450-foot drop, a camera fixed on his helmet and a parachute strapped to his back, Oberh steadies his friend, holding on to the tower for support. 'October is a windy month and that could have been dangerous for the jump. The weather guys had told me that winds start picking up at sunrise and so I had decided to do the jump at first light,' recounts Satyendra. A day before the jump, he had climbed up to the platform around the same time and sat there for close to two hours to get a feel of the place and steady his nerves.

The night before the jump has been very windy and he has toyed with the idea of calling it off, but when morning comes and he has climbed up the tower, he notices that the winds have died down. Standing on the platform, as his friend Oberh utters a loud cry of 'India!', Satyendra stifles all life-preservation instincts and throws himself off the tower. Even as the media and Army crowd gathered down below watch with bated breath, he drops 200 feet in the first three seconds before launching his parachute. 'Once my parachute opened, I was home safe. I had done 1,500 jumps by then and there were no fears any more,' he says.

'There were so many challenges in doing that jump,' he remembers. It took him a year just to get permission from the Ministry of Information and Broadcasting who couldn't understand why anyone would want to jump from there. They were also afraid that if an accident happened, it would put them in a bad light. 'I went and trained for the jump in Kuala Lumpur where the Kuala Lumpur tower was almost identical in shape, though taller, keeping in mind that a shorter tower increased the risk of my parachute not opening in time. I also needed a very brave metal-smith to fix a sturdy jump platform at that height,' he smiles. Eventually, everything came together perfectly and he set a new national record. Wingsuit flying was the next frontier to be conquered.

Flying like a bird

Satyendra traces his interest in wingsuit flying to a BASE jumping training trip to the US. 'I heard that a wingsuit training was being conducted nearby and immediately signed up for a weekend course,' he says. 'Wingsuit flying is essentially tracking in the air. Instead of falling, you glide in a particular direction using gravity.' The experience was so interesting that he was immediately hooked. When he flew back to India, a few days later, Satyendra had blown up his allowance on a brand-new bat suit that he had picked up for USD 700. The Mahim Bay flight followed and also participation in the first FAI Wingsuit Performance Flying World Cup in Netheravon, US, where he held all records for Asian participants in the year 2015.

So does the man who does so many death-defying things so effortlessly ever get scared? 'Many times,' he laughs. 'To be honest, doing anything for the first time is always scary. The key is to be prepared, take every possible precaution and yet be ready for unknown situations. That is what drives up my adrenaline and makes it all worthwhile.'

And what does adventure mean to him? 'It means taking on physical and mental challenges with due precaution but without the associated physical fear,' he says. 'I have very limited experience of combat in the Army but enough to say that coming face-to-face with an insurgent in counter-insurgency operations is the biggest adventure for any youngster. Whatever adventure sport we do in the Army—whether we are jumping from a plane, riding wild waves or climbing Mount Everest—the end purpose is to be fearless in the service of our motherland.'

Satyendra took voluntary retirement from the Army in 2013, which he had then joked with me, was to fulfil his dream of growing long bushy sideburns. He now works with the Internet and Mobile Association of India while pursuing an independent career as a skydiving, wingsuit and BASE jumping professional; and has been disappointing me each time we meet by turning up in the same old haircut. In these years, there is a lot that he has achieved. In 2014–15, he was a recipient of the Tenzing Norgay National Adventure Award. He is also the face of adventure for Mountain Dew's Real Heroes campaign. You might have seen him in print advertisements, on Mountain Dew bottle stickers and skydiving across your television screen as a wingsuit flier in their ad films.

'*Toh kya dar ke aage jeet hai?* (So does victory lie beyond fear?)' I ask, teasing him with the catch-line of the drink he models for. 'To put your life in danger from time to time breeds a saneness in dealing with day-to-day trivialities,' he smiles, quoting English aeronautical engineer Nevil Shute. That's a good quote to finish with so I decide to end the interview there and switching off my dictaphone, shift my attention to the chocolate brownie dessert that seems to have magically arrived before me and looks wickedly tempting.

6

'My missing finger is
my mountaineering trophy.'

Lieutenant Colonel Ranveer Singh Jamwal, VSM, from the JAT regiment, three-time Everest summiteer, on how a young boy from Jammu, who joined the Army as a soldier, rose to become an officer and a famous mountaineer.

25 April 2015, 11.55 a.m.
Khumbu Glacier

In the vast expanse of icy wilderness, a young, stocky mountaineer is slowly and painstakingly making his way up, one careful step at a time. His men are behind him in single file. The mountaineers are on their way to Mount Everest and trudging along slowly in sub-zero temperature when suddenly, without a warning, the earth starts moving under their feet. Looking up in alarm, they see the mountains shaking. The vision is so frightening that it strikes terror in their hearts.

The place is so barren that there is nowhere to hide and right before their frightened eyes, the mountains start caving in.

Spread over seventeen kilometres between Mount Everest and the Lhotse–Nuptse ridge, the Khumbu Glacier is a jagged sea of ice. It is the highest and fastest-moving glacier in the world and considered one of the most dangerous places in the world. Major Ranveer Singh Jamwal and his team are caught there in the infamous 2015 earthquake that left behind a heart-breaking trail of death and devastation.

* * *

September 2016
Sena Bhawan, Delhi

Ever smiling and handsome Ranveer Singh Jamwal, VSM, aka Jammy, now a Lieutenant Colonel, meets me at the Army Adventure Wing office in Delhi, where he is presently posted. He uses his hands a lot while explaining how he has climbed a dozen different peaks around the world, including the king of them all—the Everest, which he has climbed, not once, not twice, but a record number of three times. Strangely enough, I don't notice the missing finger till he holds his hand out to me, calling it his mountaineering trophy, lost to frostbite. He is happy to share his bittersweet tale of loss and achievement.

But, before that, he completes for me the happenings of the terrible day in Nepal when the earthquake hit him and his team on the Khumbu Glacier. He confesses that it remains the scariest memory of his life. 'The vision was so frightening that it struck terror even in the strongest heart. I am not a novice climber but I admit that it shook me up completely by its sheer ferociousness, even though I had seen some bad avalanches before.'

Surrounded by wall-mounted pictures of the various adventures Army persons have undertaken over the years, Jamwal recounts the happenings of that terrible day. 'Since there was no place to hide or take shelter, we just stayed in buddy pairs and watched the mayhem all around,' he says. 'Once the earth had stopped shaking, we started a slow descent. It was a miracle that all of us were safe.'

25 April 2015
A day of terror

Composing himself, Jamwal tells his men not to panic. It is not easy to move down a seventy-degree gradient. The crevasses are covered with snow and one wrong move can send a man plunging to a painful death. The temperature has dropped still further and winds are raging. Nevertheless, the resilient team makes its way down to the Base Camp, taking forty minutes to cover two kilometres.

When they walk into the camp like a pack of white ghosts covered by snow that is freezing on their bodies, they are shocked to find it almost completely destroyed. 'Most tents had been blown away. Chairs and radio sets were lying around. No one knew how many people were dead; those alive were running around crying for help,' Jamwal remembers. Those who have survived are making their way down in terrible fear that another earthquake might wipe out the rest of them too.

The first human response is to get down to safety as soon as possible but Jamwal and his team don't. Looking around, they find that two of their tents are still intact. These contain rations and medicines. Jamwal tells his men that this is a signal from above. 'I told them we would not run like cowards—we would stay back and help those in need,' says Jamwal. None of the soldiers disagree. 'That,' he says, 'is the greatness of the Army. We have been trained to be tough and resilient, and it shows in difficult times.' So, the first thing the Army team does is to shake the snow out of the fallen Tricolour and set it standing again. Then, with the flag waving in the freezing winds at 17,000 feet, they set about helping people. But before that, Jamwal passes the satellite phone around and gives each man five seconds to call home and tell his family that he is safe.

'If God has not killed us so far, he will not kill us now . . .'

Jamwal and his men begin rescue operations. Major Ritesh Goyal from the Army Medical Corps (AMC), the team doctor, stays up nights with his team of four soldiers, attending to the injured. The rest of them set up their tents, pulling bits and pieces out, go looking for those buried under snow, distribute food and medicines to the weak and injured. Sporadically, there are scary rumours of another earthquake and that the Khumbu Glacier is coming down but Jamwal tells his boys, 'If God has not killed us so far, he will not kill us now. I'm here with you, and we will not be cowards and run down. We will help the others.'

For fifteen days, Jamwal and his team stay at the Base Camp. With the Tricolour flying outside their tent, they go looking for survivors, give them first aid and food and send them down to safety. Once they are satisfied that everyone who can be helped has been helped, they start cleaning up garbage and wreckage and carry 3000 kilograms of it down to Namche Bazaar, winning a lot of appreciation from the Sagarmatha Pollution Control Committee that works for the development of Nepal. David Breashears, an American mountaineer, author and film director, who has climbed the Everest seven times and summited it five times, is also around at the Base Camp. He is so impressed with the Army team that he comes over and requests them to have a cup of tea with him. He hands over autographed DVDs to them and leaves after complimenting them on their great work. 'We were the last ones to come back,' Jamwal says, confessing that saving lives gave a bigger high than the summit ever did.

Offering me a cup of tea, Colonel Jamwal then moves on to his second story—the one where he got his unique mountaineering trophy, as he calls it. This happened six years before his scary Everest encounter while summiting the 7,272-metre high Mana peak in Uttarakhand.

May 2009, 4 a.m.
Mana summit camp

The weather is crystal clear when young Major Jammy and his team leave from the last camp for the Mana summit. The stars are twinkling in the sky as the mountaineers begin their ascent. 'The good weather had us in great spirits and there was a lot of enthusiasm when we started climbing the 400-metre wall of ice that would lead us to Mana,' recounts Jamwal, nostalgia writ large on his face. 'When we reached the edge of the ridge at 6 a.m., we were surprised to find the weather worsening.'

He tells me that big glaciers are capable of creating their own weather, and that is why even though the weather department had predicted a sunny day, dark clouds had started looming large over their worried heads. 'The summit was just 300 metres away,' says Jamwal wistfully. 'Thirty-five days of hard work had gone into reaching this point, but the sky was only getting angrier and angrier.'

He confesses there was a big temptation to not give up and go on but the real reason he and his team do not turn back is that the blizzard had buried the ropes they had tied on the way up. 'There was no way we could have risked climbing down without ropes so we decided to go up,' he says.

By 9 a.m., the temperature has dropped to minus twenty-five degrees celcius and a chill factor has set in. The men are shivering even as they climb. 'We had started feeling numbness in our hands. Walking on the inner glacier and fixing ropes had started to take its toll. We had to take off our outer gloves frequently and the inner ones had gotten wet.' Around 11 a.m. he is convinced he has frostbite in one finger. Keeping it to himself he decides to go on with his team. At 1 p.m., the men summit Mana, smiling widely despite the cold and discomfort.

Since their old ropes are lost in the snow, they put in another set of ropes and rappel down 300 metres to finally return to their camp at 8 p.m. 'We had suffered seventeen hours of exposure,' Jamwal says. He immediately starts first aid procedures by putting his finger in warm water but confesses that he knew right then that his finger had gone. And that's how our hero lost the ring finger of his left hand. But other than getting him to shift his wedding ring to his other hand, it made no difference to his life. In six months, he was back doing what he loved the most.

He joined the Army as a soldier

Jamwal did not join the Army as an officer; and he tells me this with a schoolboy grin and laughter in his eyes when he spots surprise on my face. 'Yes, Ma'am, I joined as a soldier, just like my father and my grandfather had before me,' he says. When he tells me his story, I am amazed how the Army enables people to rise from the ranks if they are really motivated and have the zeal to work hard. Inspired by his grandfather and father, Jamwal decided early in life that it was the only career for him. This young Dogra boy from Jammu, with dreams of wearing the olive-green uniform, wrote the National Defence Academy entrance exam, wanting to join the Army as an officer, but unfortunately, he did not pass.

'When I couldn't get through NDA, I decided to join the Army as a soldier. *Mujhe Army mein hi jaana tha,*' he says and that is exactly what he did at the age of seventeen-and-a-half. He joined the Army as a soldier and was sent to an infantry unit. He was there from 1994 to 1997 December. In between, Jamwal gave the Union Public Service Commission (UPSC) Army Cadet College (ACC) exam and was selected to be trained as an officer. He joined the ACC in 1998 and passed out in 2002. When he went home, proudly wearing two stars on each shoulder and saluted his thrilled grandfather, the entire family was elated. But nobody knew then that Lieutenant Ranveer Singh Jamwal was headed for some really high places on the planet as well as in life.

Jamwal joined the Jat regiment as an officer. He says that itself was a big achievement and he never thought about becoming a mountaineer till he was detailed for a course at the High Altitude Warfare School (HAWS) in Gulmarg from his battalion. Despite no previous exposure to mountaineering, he was judged best student there, and was soon sent for another skiing course. In 2006, he was posted to HAWS, but this time as an instructor of skiing and mountaineering. Soon after that, he was sent for a search-and-rescue course to Switzerland.

Conquering mountains around the world

'Going to Switzerland changed my thinking completely,' he says. 'I had never been out of the country before that. Thanks to the Army, I was now a mountaineer heading for Switzerland. It was a beautiful first exposure. We went around the entire countryside learning rescue skills. They took us to the mountainous regions and to the Swiss–Italian border. Helicopters would drop us at the top of mountains, we learnt a lot and I also got to see such a beautiful part of the world,' Jamwal says.

After he came back, he put his training to use and started leading small expeditions to places like Machoi in Kashmir and Mana in Uttarakhand, where he lost his finger, but came back hungry to climb every mountain that crossed his path. Since then, he has been on many Army expeditions. In 2012, he was selected as deputy leader of an Everest expedition. Soon after that, in September, 2012 he did an Indo-Kazakh expedition with the Kazakh army and some time later a joint expedition with a British team. Concurrently, Jammy also took on a personal challenge. He decided he would do the Seven Summits, which is considered a big achievement by mountaineers across the world. He started taking on the highest mountains of the seven continents one by one. In 2010, he went to Africa where he climbed Mount Kilimanjaro; in 2011, he climbed Aconcagua in Argentina; in 2014, he conquered Mount Elbrus in Russia, considered the highest mountain in Europe; and in 2015, he climbed the Cartsenesz Pyramid or Puncak Jaya on the Australian continental shelf.

When I finally close this story a few months later and look for Colonel Jamwal for some clarifications desired by the book editor, his phone is switched off and my messages go unread for many hours. At last there is a ping and I check my cell eagerly, hoping it is from him. 'Sorry for the late reply, Ma'am,' it says, 'It is 3 a.m. in Seattle. I shall be catching a flight to Alaska in a few hours. From there the climb to Mount Denali starts. I am ticking off the next of the Seven Summits.' He then goes on to patiently clear all my doubts.

I wish Jammy luck and get back to my copy, remembering the parting sentence he had thrown at me during that interview at Sena Bhawan. 'I have climbed twenty-four mountains in five continents so far, Ma'am. *Par, kya karun, ye dil mange more!*'

7

'We could have died on that expedition—but we didn't.'

Colonel Anand Swaroop, SM**, from Engineering Regiment, recipient of the Tenzing Norgay National Award for Land Adventure, talks about his team's skiing expedition to the South Pole.

7 May 1998
On way to Mount Panchchuli, Kumaon

Nine gutsy mountaineers from the Indian Army are on their way to Mount Panchchuli II at 22,000 feet, when they get caught in bad weather. Low clouds and heavy snowfall force them to stay closeted inside their claustrophobic tents. For two days, they can't step out in the freezing cold that has seeped right into their bones. They have also started showing signs of starvation. Now, with all rations finished, they are left with two choices: either they remain inside braving hunger and thirst till the bad weather lasts, which they know from experience, could be for days at end; or they try to find their way back in near zero visibility. With that comes the risk of exposure to the howling winds, snow-blindness, frostbite and of falling into the gaping mouths of bottomless crevasses. Expedition leader Captain Anand Swaroop takes a tough call. He decides they will go down.

They realize, soon after stepping out, that they are hopelessly lost. An avalanche takes away their gloves, shoes and sunglasses, leaving many of them at the mercy of the weather. Wrapping exposed parts of the body with whatever clothing is available, tied to each other by ropes, the mountaineers wander aimlessly on the steep slope, tired, dejected and hungry. But they haven't run out of bad luck yet. All at once, the ice below them gives way, leaving them precariously balanced on two spikes of crampons deeply entrenched in a lower sheet of ice. If even one of them trips, he will take the entire team hurtling down to a painful death thousands of feet below. Mercifully, no one does and using ice axes to secure their weight, all nine of them manage to pull themselves up to safety. Eventually, there is a gap in the cloud cover and the exhausted mountaineers reach their camp. It has been three days since they went missing. They had been assumed dead.

* * *

More than ten years later, I chance to meet the quiet and unassuming Colonel Anand Swaroop, SM**, in the Engineers Officers Mess in Delhi. He tells me, over a cup of tea, how that near-death experience changed the way he looked at life. 'We should have died during that expedition, but we didn't,' Swaroop says, a smile playing on his lips, as if he is talking about someone else. 'That day onwards I started believing in destiny—that there is a time and date fixed for each one of us. Nothing can touch us before that.' And with that learning, he says, came empowerment. He had no fears any more. And so, instead of scaring him into staying home, the Panchchuli incident egged him on to climb more mountains. Proud peaks that could give him a crick in the neck when he looked up at them but could never again shake his faith.

A very modest man, Swaroop has an impressive resume. You run out of fingers ticking off expeditions he has taken to awe-inspiring mountains including Mount Everest, Cho Oyu, Annapurna-I, Kalindi, Nanda Devi and Mana. However, the story he tells me for this book is of another frontier altogether. It is a story that unfolds on the vast, expansive stretch of ice that lesser mortals are satisfied seeing on globes, world atlases and dinnertime programmes on National Geographic—the glorious South Pole. It is the story of grit and determination and a group of adventurers who start from the coast of Antarctica and ski a distance of 1,170 kilometres in forty-nine days and ten hours to hoist the Indian flag at its very end on 15 January 2011, to mark Army Day.

The daring expedition charts the same route that Great Britain's Captain Robert Falcon Scott and his four colleagues followed in 1912 from which they never returned, perishing in snowstorms on the way back to their base camp. 'Adventurers take failed expeditions as a challenge. It is our way of honouring the ones who endeavoured but did not make it,' Swaroop tells me that evening at the Engineers Officers Mess. And then he recounts his own adventure—the 2010 Indian Army Ski Expedition to the South Pole that, he says, started with eight men in red-and-black snowsuits with the determination to man-haul sledges in minus forty degree celsius temperatures. And ended with a bath at Hotel Diego de Almagro in Punta Arenas, the southernmost town of Chile, after forty-nine long days of the bravehearts having lived in the same clothes. Here is Swaroop's story.

A journey to the end of the world

26 November 2010
Antarctica

Eight men smile widely (or as widely as Army decorum would allow), posing for a photo against the clear blue sky at the Hercules Inlet in Antarctica. A lukewarm orange sun is hanging in the horizon, and that is where it will constantly stay for the duration of the expedition since it is now the period of six months of continuous daytime at Antarctica. Picture taken, the men put on their sunglasses and skis and, staying in a single file, start their long trek to the South Pole, pulling along sledges that hold necessities that will support them over the next fifty days. These include dehydrated food, dry fruits, popcorn, foldable stoves running on aviation turbine fuel, one-litre thermos flasks to store water made from melting snow every morning, tents, medicines, music players, e-books on pen drives, a satellite phone and a solar panel to charge it.

They follow a set routine every day. Getting up at 7 a.m. every morning, they put on their down jackets, fold their tents and after a breakfast of dehydrated food heated on the stoves that they carry, they start the day's trek at 9 a.m. The men walk in a single file, the first sledge carrying the Tricolour standing out in the stark expanse of white all around. They ski for almost eight hours every day, stopping every hour to take a ten-minute break. Their constant companion is the sun that is always hanging at the horizon. Despite its presence, at 7 p.m. every day, they call it a day and after pitching their tents, quickly change their sweat-soaked socks to avoid frostbite. They get used to their gloved hands and feet inside woollen socks getting painful pinpricks from the sweat that tends to freeze into sharp needles because of the cold.

'When we started the expedition, everything was new to us,' says Swaroop. 'Though we had the best equipment and good training, the weather was an always an uncertainty. We never realized how tough it was to pull sledges in blizzards and over blue ice in freezing temperatures. Sometimes, the wind would drop down to zero kilometres per hour, and sometimes it would whip up howling blizzards moving at 100 kilometres an hour.' The adventurers endure it all. Their training in Greenland has prepared them for the expedition but they quickly realize that skiing is a lot more difficult when it comes down to doing it on ice with thickness varying from 3,000 feet at the coast, from where they begin their expedition, to 10,000 feet at the pole, where they end it. 'Even navigation was difficult. A compass was used by the leading man but at the poles even magnetic fields don't behave correctly,' explains Swaroop. It is amusing for those at the back of the line to see the lead man skiing at an angle while he thinks he is going straight.

A strange birthday cake

They undergo a trying time when Lance Naik Khilap Singh, official photographer of the expedition, develops a boil under one eye. In two days, it has become so big that he cannot keep his eye open. Sunburn and ultraviolet rays are only making it worse. Besides not being able to see properly, he is also suffering excruciating pain. With no doctor having volunteered for the expedition, Rifleman Tsewang Morup fills in and starts giving him painkillers. 'We were really worried about Khilap but on the third night, the boil broke on its own and he quickly got better,' says Swaroop.

There are happy times too. They celebrate the birthday of Lance Naik Parsuram Gurung of the phenomenal haircutting skills, who is responsible for keeping the men looking smartly trimmed even in the wilds of the South Pole. A cake is shaped out of halwa and dry fruits, and cut by the birthday boy to lusty clapping all around. The enthusiasm of the men remains unabated even in the toughest of situations and for this Swaroop gives credit to the sheer positivity of the team members. A quality highly overrated while picking volunteers for adventure missions is physical fitness, he says. 'A person needs to be fit but what matters most in the end is his attitude. A positive attitude helps you take on every difficulty as a challenge. It makes the difference between carrying on and giving up and often between life and death,' he says.

Finally, South Pole

The expedition leaves the men with many memories that shall be cherished for a lifetime. These include camping close to the isolated Thiel mountains and crossing over sastrugi (dunes formed by wind erosion of hard snow), rushing to get inside their tents while waiting for blizzards to die down and moving out when the winds are gentler. The days pass and the men finally make it to the South Pole (90 degrees S, 0 degrees W) on 15 January 2011, placing India on the adventure map of Antarctica for time immemorial. They hoist the Army flag and the Tricolour there and then take a chartered Twin Otter plane back to Punta Arenas. After fifty long days of living off the land, they finally relax in the plush Hotel Diego de Almagro, where they feel soap on their skin and shampoo in their matted hair. They sing along to music from their Walkmans, place pen drives back in their pockets and reminisce about phone calls made to loved ones from the abject whiteness of the West Antarctic Ice Sheet. They soak in the luxury till its time for Republic Day celebrations at the Indian Embassy in Santiago, following which they fly back to New Delhi for a well-deserved handshake with the Army Chief. And that is how one of the most interesting adventures of Colonel Anand Swaroop's life ends.

The boy with an eighteen-gear bicycle

'Life is either a daring adventure or nothing at all.' Swaroop likes to quote Helen Keller and says that it applies aptly to his life too. A bicycle introduced him to adventure, he tells me. When he was fifteen, and studying in St Francis College, Lucknow, a cousin who was serving in the Merchant Navy gifted him an eighteen-gear bicycle that he fell hopelessly in love with.

'I immediately started looking for excuses to go out of the house. It would include going to and coming back from school, attending tuitions, getting stuff for my mother and volunteering for any chore anyone had that needed to be done outside the house,' he laughs, 'I would sometimes cycle as much as fifty kilometres a day.'

In Class IX, Swaroop enrolled for the junior wing of the National Cadet Corps and started attending camps that introduced him to rifle shooting and flying gliders. The NCC also sent him for a basic mountaineering course to Darjeeling and a cycling expedition from Lucknow to Delhi which he extended all the way to Shimla on his own, shocking his parents completely. 'I even managed a trip to Bhutan on a shoestring budget after my mountaineering course. I think all these were symptoms of being bitten by the adventure bug though at that time I just found it fun to go and do these things.' He slowly realized that adventure made his life worthwhile and, after graduation, the Army became an obvious choice of career. 'I didn't know much about it then but I knew that it offered an adventurous way of life,' he says.

He joined the Corps of Engineers and went on to lead many mountaineering expeditions. Often, he says, he had to barter his annual leave for an expedition. 'Had I got my leave, I would have still packed my bags and headed for the mountains so it really made no difference,' he laughs. He confesses that he was so caught up in this serious relationship with nature that he never got around to getting married. 'I kept getting these opportunities to do exciting things and my life was just too complete to consider shifting to a normal routine,' he says.

However, he continues to travel and climb in his holidays. 'There are so many adventures waiting to be undertaken; like skiing to both the poles in the same calendar year, sailing around the world, doing a road trip around the globe climbing the highest peaks of all the continents,' he says, 'I plan to do some of that after I retire and have more time. The fun is certainly not over yet.'

8

'On Everest, mental fortitude counts more than physical strength.'

Major Deepika Rathore, VSM, from the Army Ordnance Corps; two-time Everest summiteer shares her experience of climbing the Everest and meeting dead people on the way.

May 2016
On way to Everest Camp 3

A team of National Cadet Corps (NCC) girl cadets between the ages of eighteen and twenty-two is slowly making its way from Everest Camp 2 to Camp 3. They look up at the icy Lhotse wall, a snow-covered seventy-five-degree incline that stands 4000 feet high. There is a howling sound and rocks come pelting down at them. The girls watch their heads, hold on to their ropes firmly and continue to climb. All of a sudden, a pair of gloves and a water bottle come tumbling down the steep incline. The startled girls look up to find something heavier rolling past. They are confused but their team leader Major Deepika Rathore's experienced eyes have already made out a head and a pair of legs. 'It was a Sherpa who had been guiding a team of mountaineers ahead,' she says, 'He had lost his balance and we could see him fall to his death.'

That evening at Camp 3, precariously perched on a narrow icy ledge at 22,000 feet, when Deepika goes to check on the girls, she finds them scared and upset. That is when she tells them, very matter-of-factly, that spotting dead bodies on the Everest is very normal. They will find dead mountaineers who had stopped to rest for a while and never got up; dying ones who do not have the strength to move any more and are just lying there in the freezing cold waiting for life to ebb out of them; and those with high-altitude pulmonary oedema (HAPO) or High Altitude Sickness—disoriented and hallucinating because of low oxygen—often walking alone, up and down the same path or taking off their clothes because they believe they are feeling hot. Deepika shares with them experiences from her earlier climb, holds them in a group hug and tells them, 'Don't lose hope. Learn from them. They are all very good mountaineers—salute their courage and move on.'

* * *

December 2016
Jaipur

When I finally nail Major Deepika Rathore, VSM, for an interview, which is not easy since she is travelling a lot and even her mail is going unanswered, she is posted as training officer, National Cadet Corps Group Headquarters in Jaipur. Physically fit, vibrant and good-looking, she talks with great enthusiasm about her journey to becoming an Army officer. I notice that her eyes sparkle the most when she describes the adventures she has had climbing the Everest, which she has done twice. The first time when she volunteered to go on an Army expedition as a newly married young girl, and the second, when she herself led a team of NCC girl cadets. This is her inspiring story. But of course, we start with her experiences on the Everest, the most formidable of which is meeting the dead.

A frozen climber

'When you climb the Everest, you get used to running into dead people,' says Major Deepika Rathore. She recollects how on her way to the summit from Camp 4, she had sat down next to a male climber who also seemed to be resting. 'I sat there for a while, drank some water and then got up to start climbing again,' she says. When she is coming down in the morning, she realizes it is the perfectly preserved body of a climber who must have sat down to rest and could never get up again.

They say human beings are not supposed to be on the Everest and on those heights, the human body starts dying slowly. Yet, it seems to hold a fatal attraction for mountaineers who put their lives at risk and climb it time and again. 'On the Everest, mental strength counts more than physical strength,' she says. 'I guess that's true for life itself.' And we must take what this gutsy lady officer with the indomitable spirit tells us seriously because she has scaled the mightiest peak in the world twice. It becomes an even bigger achievement if we consider that she comes from Nagore village in Rajasthan where girls are expected to be coy and docile and often not encouraged to venture into male-dominated professions. Deepika says her parents always encouraged her to do what she wanted. And though she wears a veil over her face at family functions to express respect for traditions, she also recounts how it was her handsome maternal grandfather, standing proud in his uniform who was the first to inspire her to join the Army.

The scariest place in the world

May 2012
Khumbu Icefall

When I ask Deepika to share one of her unforgettable Everest memories, she relates a terrifying experience she had on Khumbu Glacier on way to the summit. 'I was twenty-six years old and part of an all-women Army officers' expedition, which was my first to Everest,' she says. 'We had left Base Camp and were on Khumbu, the highest glacier in the world.' Deepika says she remembers Khumbu as one of the scariest places in the world. 'A vast expanse of white, it is totally covered with ice. A mountaineer does not know if she is stepping on a crevasse at her next step or if an avalanche is headed her way. All climbers go to Khumbu with a prayer on their lips and just concentrate on getting out of there as quickly as they can.'

While the team is crossing Khumbu Icefall, considered one of the most dangerous obstacles on the route to the Everest, they spot a Sherpa just ahead. Deepika remembers having seen him before. He is an Everest veteran who has summited more than eight times, she recollects. Seemingly distracted and in a hurry, he steps on the aluminium ladder fixed like a bridge across a big gaping crevasse and Deepika marvels at how easily he seems to be doing it from sheer muscle memory alone. Then all of a sudden, before her horrified eyes, the Sherpa loses his balance and falls into the gaping depths. Right in front of Deepika's horrified eyes, his body shatters on the rocks below and his blood splashes all over the white snow.

'That is my scariest Everest memory,' she says. 'When it was my turn to step on the ladder to cross the same crevasse, I had tears of shock and grief in my eyes and my legs were shaking in fear. Down below I could see the Sherpa's blood splattered on the ice, and I was trembling so much that I thought I would be the next to go,' she says. But she managed to steel her mind and move on.

Climbing Everest the second time

May 2016

Deepika's team, comprising ten girl cadets, one junior commissioned officer (JCO) and two non-commissioned officers (NCOs), starts from Jiri village in Nepal, just off the Kathmandu highway. Since most Everest expeditions—

including the one that put Tenzing Norgay and Edmund Hillary on the summit—passed through Jiri, it is called the 'Gateway to Mount Everest'. The girls take seventeen days to reach the Everest Base Camp. There, at 17,500 feet, they find a crazy mix of sights, sounds and accents—colourful tents, music and climbers from across the globe are everywhere. Almost every language in the world can be heard here; satellite phones buzz; piping hot food gets cold faster than you can eat it; freshly washed hair can freeze in strange shapes and you are often lulled to sleep by the sound of ice cracking up in the mountain that looms before you like a giant that must be tamed. Over the next nine days, the team undergoes the complete acclimatization schedule, going right up to Camp 3 at 23,000 feet and returning to Base Camp. There, they wait for a weather window to begin their summit attempt.

18 May 2016

The clearance finally comes. The girls get up at midnight, freshen up, and after choosing from a generous choice of breakfast that includes porridge, boiled eggs, upma and poha, start climbing at 1 a.m. 'You lose your appetite at that height,' explains Deepika, adding, 'In those five days, I could only eat a few energy bars.' By afternoon, around 2 p.m., after a long uphill climb across the ever-moving Khumbu Icefall, they reach Camp 2, which has been set up in a rocky area, at the foot of the Lhotse wall. Clouds come right into their tents and the girls get their last hot cooked meal. Here onwards the girls have to manage on pre-cooked food that they force themselves to consume even though the urge to eat is getting less with each step. They try to catch up on sleep but at that altitude, it is very difficult to relax so much that you can close your eyes and sleep.

The next morning, they start for Camp 3 at 6.30 a.m., crossing the tricky Lhotse wall with its steep incline and constant threat of falling rocks and ice blocks. They make their second night's halt at the steeply perched camp, where going to the toilet in the night is in itself an ordeal. Harsh winds howl in their ears even as they rest and prepare to start early the next morning.

The Death Zone

On the third day, the girls start from Camp 3, reaching Camp 4 at 4 p.m. Also called the Death Zone, at 28,000 feet Camp 4 is situated on what looks like a white jagged moonscape. The sky is a deep cobalt blue and the steep, stark white climb to the final summit stares them in the face. By now, temperatures have dropped further, the air is thinner and the girls are already fatigued. They are advised an increased intake of water to combat dehydration. They try to rest in their pup tents but most can't because of the excitement and fear. They think of their families and friends and lie there in anticipation of what lies ahead.

At 9 p.m., they begin the final summit. 'It was dark when we started from Camp 4, which is also called the summit camp,' says Deepika. The mountaineers have their headlamps on. Those who trail behind see the narrow arch of light moving ahead as the initial climbers slowly wind their way up in the dark. Each member has a Sherpa to guide and assist them and also carry two oxygen cylinders for each member. It soon starts snowing and as the snowflakes fall on them, the team plods ahead slowly in the night, placing one weary foot after another. A dull moon rises behind them.

'Snow was flying all around us, the wind chill factor had increased and the exhausting climb seemed almost endless,' recounts Deepika. The team walks for five and a half hours, their progress careful and slow. At 2.30 a.m., the lead climbers reach the South Summit. From here they know that the final summit is just 800 metres away. They wait there for the slower ones. 'We spent an hour there so that the team could be together. Our bodies started getting colder. I had started shivering while we waited and kept stomping my feet to keep my blood flowing,' Deepika says. She knows that as long as she keeps walking the blood will keep circulating, which decreases chances of frostbite.' She suffers a setback when her Sherpa tells her that he is feeling unwell and wants to go back to camp. Determined to make it with her team, Deepika lets him go, deciding to stay back with the girls. 'I knew I had to climb to the summit with them—I was their biggest hope.'

The summit

21 May 2016

Once the team is together, they start the final climb to the top. A narrow, jagged ridge looks them in the face—it is the

Knife Ridge, the final obstacle in their path with Hillary's Step somewhere in between. Deepika is doing it for the second time but she knows that in the Everest, each experience is new. She pulls herself up carefully, breathing heavily with each step. At 10.30 a.m., she is almost at the summit. Below her, the clouds float. She sits down in the freezing cold and takes out the mobile phone that she has carefully wrapped in woollen socks to preserve the battery.

'I took a selfie and noticed that my cheeks were wet with tears,' she says, smiling nostalgically. 'It seemed as if I was with God.'

For thirty minutes, Deepika sits alone at 29,029 feet, the highest point in the world, controlling her tears, because she knows how precious body water is on the Everest. Her mind goes back to the year 2011 when she had reached the summit at 5 a.m. on a cold and windy day. 'I couldn't stand there for five minutes then,' she remembers. 'Our cameras didn't work because of the cold. The only tangible memory I have of that summit is one solo picture and one group photograph taken by the Discovery Channel photographer, who was following our expedition.'

She is still in her thoughts when thirty minutes later, the first girl cadet, nineteen-year-old Lalritaungi from Mizoram, walks up followed by Havildar Balram Singh. Lalritaungi hugs Deepika and breaks into tears. Deepika tells her they are still a little below the summit. They have to walk for five more minutes. One by one, the other girls join them. By 11.45 a.m., the team is together and they climb up to the summit. It is a clear day and down below they can see the swirling clouds and the lower peaks of Makau, Makalu, Lhotse and Kanchenjunga poking their heads out of their misty folds. They sparkle white where the sun is falling on them and blue and grey in the shadows. The wind screams in their ears but it is temporarily drowned in the music of their own achievement. Spending about fifty minutes at the top, huddled together on the pool table length of the summit, they start their descent. On their way down, where the views are the best, they stretch out their arms, certain that they can touch the sky but can actually only grab bits of limestone from the rocky areas they cross.

On the way down, Deepika starts feeling exhausted and dehydrated, both extremely dangerous conditions in the mountain. She tries to open a two-litre flask of water that she is carrying but her fingers can't do it. She makes ice balls and sucks on them willing herself to put one foot in front of another. She knows that the maximum number of accidents happen on the way down, when the body is tired and the weather starts packing up. The team reaches South Col at 3 p.m. and decides to halt there for the night. They fall into their tents exhausted. The next morning, they start the long walk back to Base Camp. It is there that they can finally sleep the undisturbed sleep of relief, but they still can't because they are exhilarated by the thought that they have scaled Everest. It is a place they will revisit many times in their conversations and their dreams.

Deepika's Journey

Deepika comes from a middle-class family with their roots in the village of Nagore in Rajasthan, and was born and brought up in Jaipur. I find it pleasantly surprising that a girl from one of the most traditional parts of India dreamt of being an Army officer and made it too. Deepika laughs at my question. 'My father is a manager in a government bank and my mother is a homemaker,' she says, 'But my inspiration to join the Army came from my maternal grandfather Captain S.S. Shekhawat who was with the President's Bodyguards (PBG). When I was a little girl, I would see him wearing the uniform and I just decided I wanted to join the Army as well.'

Deepika studied in Shri Bhawani College where she joined the NCC and the wish to join the Army became stronger. 'I did mountaineering courses and some expeditions with the NCC and slowly, like most other mountaineers, climbing the highest mountain in the world became a dream.' In 2004, she went for a basic mountaineering course to the Nehru Institute of Mountaineering in Uttarkashi, and in 2005 she got the chance to climb Mount Thelu at 20,000 feet. After that, there was no looking back. And though she didn't know it then, Mount Everest was just around the corner.

In April 2011, just a month and a half after she got married, Deepika was posted in Nimmu, Leh, when she came across an official circular that an all-women's expedition was being planned to the Everest for which volunteers were invited. 'It had always been my dream to scale the Everest. I discussed it with my husband who told me I must go,' she says. Her application was accepted. And that was how the little girl with sparkling eyes who would look at her handsome Nanaji in his crisp uniform and spit-shined boots and tell everyone she wanted to wear the olive-green uniform as well, became not just an Army officer but an accomplished mountaineer too. Deepika's story holds a message for everyone, particularly for girls who are often pushed to stay within gender-defined roles. Don't be afraid to dream. Dreams do come true.

Army Adventure Wing—A temple for adventurers

To find out how teenagers with dreams of adventure turn into the Army's bravehearts like mountaineer Lieutenant Colonel Ranveer Singh Jamwal, microlight flier Lieutenant Colonel Ujjwal Panchal, hot air balloonist Lieutenant Colonel Durig Kishen and so many others you need to visit the Army Adventure Wing (AAW) at Sena Bhawan, New Delhi. This is the Army's one-stop shop from where you can go anywhere in the world for any kind of adventure, right from river rafting in the Zanskar river to mountain terrain biking to skydiving to climbing Mount Everest to driving in competitive car rallies like the Raid de Himalaya. Being an officer in the Indian Army is probably the only profession in India that gives you a salary for pursuing the adventure activity you are passionate about and lets you do it in your work hours.

Adventure has always been an integral part of the Indian Army. It is believed that it helps in fostering the qualities of courage, conviction, purpose and camaraderie, all of which are important in daily life and even more so in times of war. The Army needs young men who will be brave, whose self-belief will not shake in times of adversity, who will stand by their men even at risk of death, and adventure nurtures all these. The AAN plans, coordinates and conducts all major adventure projects the Army undertakes. These include adventures on land, in air and on water. It also conducts inter-services adventure activities like parasailing, bicycle tours or low-altitude treks at a national and even international level.

How do officers volunteer?

Experts like Jamwal are posted to the AAW in Delhi and look after its three branches: aero, aqua and land. Each branch has an officer in charge and handles a particular type of adventure. The aim is to help and guide young officers who want to pursue a particular adventure and see that they get an opportunity to participate. If a particular officer performs really well, she or he is noticed and given further opportunities to pursue the sport and finally, the chance to even become an instructor in their chosen field.

The AAW organizes hundreds of adventure activities annually. These could include a trek, a river-rafting expedition, a sailing trip around the world or an Everest expedition. The announcement is made on the Army intranet, a private site accessible to all Army officers, and circulars are sent to all formations and units. Volunteers need to fill up a form and send it to the AAW. Once the vacancies are filled up for a particular activity, a wait list is created and most people who don't get selected the first time, get their chance the next time. Each adventure activity has a node where it is carried out. For instance, blue water sailing is done in Mumbai, wind surfing in Gopalpur, scuba diving in Havelock Island in the Andamans and white-water rafting in the Zanskar and the Ganga. Highly experienced instructors are posted at each node to teach candidates all the intricacies of the sport.

All adventure activities are graded from a low to high level. Youngsters are encouraged to join at the lowest level and rise up. Anybody in the Indian Army can volunteer for any of the expeditions, though nearly all have a fifty-fifty ratio of the old guard to the young lot so that there is a right blend of experience, safety and enthusiasm.

The Incredibles

These are the stories of a General who cut off his own foot, a marathon runner who has a metal blade for a leg, a quadriplegic who flies gliders, and a paratrooper whose parachute failed to open but he lived to tell the tale.

9

'Everything in my body is broken—except my smile!'

Major D.P. Singh (Retd.), Dogra, Kargil War amputee and champion marathoner, proves that battles and bravery don't end with war. And legs aren't always made of muscles and bone.

November 2009, New Delhi
Near the Ashok Hotel, start-point of the Airtel Delhi Half Marathon

It is a clear and crisp morning. There is a slight chill in the air and palpable excitement at the venue. Enthusiastic runners— fit youngsters, senior citizens, middle-aged ladies with wide smiles and giggling kids—are gathering in the orange light of early dawn, pinning stickers on their T-shirts, devouring last-minute glucose biscuits and gearing up for the run. Just then, a car stops smoothly in the parking lot, filling the gap between two vehicles. Out steps a young Sikh gentleman with shining eyes and a carriage that suggests he might have something to do with the defence forces.

Ten years have passed since a mortar blast during the Kargil War blew off a part of Major D.P. Singh's leg, leading to gangrene and amputation from the knee downwards. Over the years he has learnt to live with a prosthetic leg. Now he wants to take it one step further. He plans to run the Airtel New Delhi Half Marathon.

Singh locks his car and walks down to the start-point in shorts and a T-shirt. That is when people start noticing his slight limp and artificial leg. He tries to look away from sympathetic eye contact but cannot ignore the sceptical 'Can-he-actually-run?' smiles. The compassionate faces of his fellow runners seem to think he can't do it. He doesn't say a word but promises himself, 'I *will* prove them wrong.' He then looks at the two chest numbers he is holding in his hand, one for the twenty-one kilometres half marathon and another for the six-kilometre run.

* * *

September 2016
Gurgaon

I ring the bell of Major D.P. Singh's Gurgaon apartment while subconsciously checking my bag to see if I have remembered to carry my dictaphone. The door opens and he is before me in a flash. Dressed in a fluorescent green T-shirt and jeans, and a bright smile on his face, he greets me with a 'Good morning, Ma'am'; the quintessential Army officer—physically fit, dignified and well-mannered. There is no sign that he wears an artificial leg. He walks around nimbly and radiates energy. It is easy to believe he is the marathon runner of the high-impact Reebok advertisement for 'Odds' or footwear with both shoes of the pair for the same foot that has left me with goose pimples a day before. If you haven't seen it already, I suggest you do. The film begins with Singh running alone under a steel bridge with Kabir Bedi's deep baritone asking: 'Odd isn't it, for a man to be running when he shouldn't even be walking? To complete a marathon on one leg, when really he should be sitting at home and watching it?' It follows him home and shows him wearing his uniform, then mentions how he survived death in a war yet still has a war to fight; and ends with the line, 'He has endured the odds. The question is, have we?'

Fact is that when Kargil War amputee Major D.P. Singh goes shopping for trainers, he looks for only one shoe. That's because his other leg is fitted with a steel blade. This is his story. He starts by telling me about the day that he ran his first half marathon.

'At the 2009 Airtel Delhi Half Marathon in 2009, I had registered for both, the twenty-one kilometres half marathon and the six-kilometre run since I wasn't sure how much I would be able to run.

'I had thought that if I manage to do fourteen kilometres in the practice runs, I will pull through the remaining seven on the day of the half marathon. Otherwise, I would run six kilometres this year and go for twenty-one the next year. But in my practice sessions, I had never been able to go beyond nine kilometres,' says Singh, handing me a cup of tea. 'But by the time I walked down to the starting point, I had received so many looks of disbelief and pity from people that it helped me make up my mind. "Ab toh chahe kuch bhi ho jaaye, main ekis kilometre hi bhagunga, (Come what may, I will only run the twenty one kilometre now.)" I decided.'

And so, Singh hop-runs the entire distance, completely ignoring the prosthetic limb rubbing against his knee at every step. He also ignores the voice in his head that is constantly coaxing him to stop, take a lift, opt for a short cut. 'All our battles are fought in the mind, between the two people who reside inside us,' he says philosophically. 'One is good and strong, and the other is bad and weak. Through the three hours and forty-nine minutes it took me to run that day, my weak self kept tempting me to give up but I knew that if I didn't do this today, I would lose all self-respect for the rest of my life.'

When he reaches the finish line, there is loud cheering. He looks up and is pleasantly surprised to find many people clapping, disbelief mingled with respect in their eyes. They are cheering and shouting and queuing up to shake hands with him. Singh meets their eyes proudly this time, a smile playing on his lips. 'It was the most amazing moment of my life—I cannot even describe how I felt,' he says. 'It was not the physical pain that I had overcome, it was the mental weakness. Winning against yourself is the most difficult thing in life and those who have won this fight have the power to change things.'

What bystanders don't know is that by this time the stump, which has constantly taken the impact of the prosthetic leg for twenty-one kilometres, has been severely lacerated.

Because of the pain, he can barely walk to his car, but he does manage to get there, dragging his leg behind him. When he finally gets home and removes his artificial leg, he finds the wound raw and bleeding. It will take a long time to heal but Singh brushes it off as yet another war injury.

15 July 1999, Kargil
A blast that changed his life

It is approximately 5.30 a.m. and Major D.P. Singh is still in bed, but preparing to get up, when an ear-shattering blast rips through the air. The ground shakes violently under his bed and a spray of metal pieces, sharp as knives, cuts into his body, pinning him down to his mattress. He doesn't know then that a mortar shell had landed right next to his tent and burst. In seconds, Singh becomes unconscious. Blood is flowing out of him like a fountain but he has no idea what is happening around him.

When the soldiers come running to his tent, they find him lying in a pool of blood. His stomach has been ripped apart by shrapnel, exposing his intestines, and all the flesh has been blown off his right leg, knee downwards, exposing the white bone. They quickly drape Singh in a blanket and carry him across to where the ambulance is waiting. He then begins the longest journey of his life; a two-and-a-half hour drive on a mud track to the closest hospital in Akhnoor. It is a sixty-kilometre ride that will take him from near-death to life. He is in excruciating pain and slipping in and out of consciousness. 'I vaguely remember my regimental medical officer (RMO) trying to keep a conversation going in order to keep me conscious through the route,' he says, 'but I fell unconscious again.'

The shocked young doctor on duty takes one look at his blood-soaked body being brought in on a stretcher and pronounces him dead on arrival, asking the soldiers to take him to the mortuary. Luckily, another doctor, an anaesthetist, happens to be around and realizes he is alive. Singh has no intention of dying and he continues to battle for his life in the Intensive Care Unit (ICU) where on the third day, the same doctor notices that gangrene is setting in in his mangled foot.

If the infected part is not cut off quickly, it will poison his whole body. A helicopter takes Singh to the Udhampur Command Hospital. Doctors there are alarmed by his condition and he is advised immediate amputation. The surgeon tells him very honestly that only in the operation theatre will he be able to decide just how much of Singh's leg can be saved. A very brave Singh tells the doctor not to worry and go ahead with the operation.

When Singh emerges from surgery, he finds that his leg has been amputated from the knee. For many days, the young Sikh with the severed leg hovers between life and death. While his family is worried sick, a tough-as-nails Singh asks for his tape recorder, disturbs other patients by playing the soundtrack of his favourite film *Sholay* and religious hymns in Gurbani in the ICU and spends time joking with the nurses. The shrapnel in his stomach has cut through his intestines and they have fused together post the injury, not letting his body digest any food. However, his sheer determination to live towers over everything else.

He is moved to the Army Research and Referral Hospital, Delhi, where intensive surgery is carried out on his stomach, removing many metres of his small intestine. After he recovers from this surgery, he is moved to the Prosthetic Limb Centre in Pune. When they weigh him in Pune, he is all of twenty-eight kilograms. But from there, he gets on the road to recovery. He finds some interesting comrades in the other veterans, also Kargil amputees, who are also being fitted with artificial limbs. 'We would crack jokes, sing songs, exchange war gossip and even visit clubs where I would dance on one leg,' remembers Singh. 'Since so many of us went through the process of losing a limb together, we used to crack jokes about it. We wore our injuries like war medals.'

Boarded out of the infantry because of his 100 per cent disability, Singh shifts to the Army Ordnance Corps in a desk job. Though he starts playing golf and even squash, he still misses the adrenaline rush of athletics. He serves for ten years and even does a car rally from Kargil to Kanyakumari in 2005 but soon starts getting frustrated. 'I had joined the Army for adventure, not to sit in an office and do paper work. So I decided to leave and pursue it on my own,' he says. In 2007, he comes out with a medical pension. Two years later, he runs his first half marathon.

The blade runner

The Airtel Half Marathon becomes a turning point in Singh's life. After that amazing hop-run, Singh finds new meaning in his life. 'The elation I felt on completing that run was incomparable to anything else in my life. This was what I wanted to do.' A few weeks later he meets the big-moustached Lieutenant General Mukesh Sabharwal, the Adjutant General, Indian Army, at the golf course. Proud of Singh's achievement, Lieutenant General Sabharwal asks, 'What can I do for you, son?'

Singh requests him for a blade that can help him run better and the General fulfils his promise. The Artificial Limb Centre is asked to import the three-and-a-half kilogram blade that will change his life. He can't wait to get it fitted and to start running. However, both goals are extremely difficult.

The blade is pure metal; it does not have any muscle or cartilage to cushion the impact of running. 'The first time I ran with it, my knee was soaked with blood. Each time I jumped and landed on the blade, a force equivalent to two-and-a-half times my body weight would be generated. The shock would travel all the way to my head.' But he doesn't let that stop him from running. In 2011, he completes his first blade half marathon, clocking a time of two hours and forty minutes. By the time he finishes, his leg has swollen so much that it is difficult to even remove the blade. For many days, he can't even get up from his bed. 'Only a fool would do it again after such a painful experience,' says Singh, adding with a grin, 'I did!' After the wound healed, he was back on the road once again. His amputated leg has become tougher over time, but even after all these years, the pain remains. 'Each time I take a step and my body weight falls on the stump that has the metal blade attached to it, I wince. The impact carries all the way up to my brain,' he tells me, 'But my sense of achievement makes up for all that. It cannot stop me from running.'

Running against all odds

Marathon running has now become his passion. He ran his first three marathons on his walking prosthetic. Thereafter, he became India's blade runner. Not content with that, he formed a group of amputees called 'The Challenging Ones'. It now has 1150 members from across the country. 'The idea is to show differently abled people that they are not the physically challenged ones—they are the challengers,' he explains. As many as 150 members of the group run in various events happening across the country. Singh himself has run more than twenty-one half marathons, including two at 12,000 feet, and on 13 January 2017, he ran a full marathon solo to celebrate his own birthday. From his first run in three hours and forty-nine minutes, he has brought down his best half marathon time to two hours and ten minutes. He holds four Limca records: he is the first amputee to run a marathon in India, the first blade runner in India, the first blade runner to run at a high altitude and has received the Limca People of the Year Award for the year 2016. He has become a role model for not just the differently abled but for every single person who has a personal battle to fight.

A long journey

Singh says he had a tough life initially. When he was in Class II, his father lost his job due to some false allegations made against him. This brought the responsibility of running the house on his mother's shoulders. Singh was sent to live with his grandparents in Roorkee. He started going to the Kendriya Vidyalaya in the cantonment where his daily walk to school through the Army area exposed him to Army life. 'I was convinced that the Army was the career for me. My grandparents had inculcated my Sikh faith within me and I always felt the Army followed the same tenets of tolerance, martyrdom and selfless sacrifice. They would step in wherever something was going wrong, make it all right and then leave quietly without any expectations,' he says.

Singh says his Army dream did come true but it had many twists in between. The first setback came when he could not pass his Class XI exams, and was not able to join the NDA. 'Whenever I meet children, I make it a point to tell them this. I like to tell them that we should never let small setbacks affect our enthusiasm to pursue our dreams,' he says. Naturally, Singh did not let these failures change anything he had planned for himself. After finishing school, he wrote an exam for bank clerks and cleared it. Moving to Ludhiana, he started working with Allahabad Bank while studying privately for his graduation. He deliberately chose history and English—subjects he was weak at—believing it would make him grasp them better. Another challenge he tried to overcome was his discomfort in speaking English. 'Since I was not at all confident about talking in English, I would stand in front of a mirror and read my English newspaper loudly every single day. It was quite amusing for my neighbour who would laugh and say, "Sardar pagal ho gaya hai! (The Sardar has gone mad!)"' But the hard work paid off eventually. After another failed attempt, Singh finally made it to the IMA and got to live his Army dream. The Kargil War interrupted it but Singh says he never questioned his faith even after the loss of his leg. 'I just told myself I was meant for higher things in life.'

Singh leads a full life, running his half marathons, organizing events for social causes, motivating the differently abled, and a lot more. Living with fifty pieces of shrapnel embedded in his body, broken ribs, hearing loss, elbow and knee injuries, a damaged liver and a damaged urinary bladder, he likes to quip, 'Everything in my body is broken except my smile!'

10

'I hit the ground from 8,500 feet with an unopened parachute.'

Major Sandesh Kadam, PARA, tells the unbelievable story of his fall from an AN 32 aircraft on the day his parachute did not open.

6 January 2010

Dressed in his regular olive-green combat uniform, parachute strapped to his back, twenty-seven-year-old Captain Sandesh Kadam from the elite PARA stands at the exit door of the aircraft ready to jump. He has a rucksack weighing twenty kilograms on his back, a dummy rifle slung on his side, and he is ready for his twenty-seventh free fall jump. Combat free falls train paratroopers to jump into enemy territory from heights above 8,000 feet with weapons, rations and ammunition so that they are self-sufficient for over seventy-two hours and can conduct operations in enemy territory.

It's a bright clear afternoon but there's a biting chill in the air. Kadam feels the draft on his face. 'Green on go,' he hears the crisp voice of the Air Force instructor. It's his signal to jump. Kadam flings himself out of the plane belly down with his arms spread out in the classical free fall pose, altimeter strapped to his left wrist. He knows that when he's at 5,000 feet, he has to throw his parachute into the air. The adrenaline rushes through his veins as he falls at a speed that goes beyond 200 miles an hour, in a spread-eagle position, the wind whipping his face, the ground coming closer every second.

The moment the altimeter touches 5,000 feet, Kadam pulls his parachute release handle and waits for the jerk that will tell him the parachute is now open and controlling his descent. It does not happen. A surprised Kadam tilts his body slightly to look up. 'I saw the nylon rigging lines up in the air and the bag with my unopened parachute floating above me,' he says. He is in a life-threatening emergency situation.

2 January 2017
Agra

Paratrooper Sandesh Kadam should not be alive. He jumped from an aircraft at 8,500 feet and when his parachute did not open, he hit the ground in twenty seconds flat, his altimeter recording a terminal velocity of more than 200 miles an hour. And yet, there he is—tall, fit and dashing, now a Major, parking his bicycle and walking around with a wide smile on his face. Unless, of course, I'm seeing a ghost! Major Sandesh

Kadam's is one of the most unbelievable survival stories you are ever likely to hear. He has defied the rules that decide what mere mortals can do, though he tends to modestly laugh it off by calling it 'just another example of the grit and spirit of a paratrooper'. Here is his story.

Kadam says the reason he did not panic that day when his parachute did not open is because he has been trained not to. He has been taught that in such conditions, he should disturb his free fall position a little and that is what he does first. He jerks the unopened bag a little, hoping that will make his parachute unfurl. Nothing happens. Meanwhile, strong air currents take over his body, twisting and turning him into what paratroopers call a barrel roll. The rigging lines wrap around his body and tighten. He is probably facing the sky now but in the vast void of the blue sky, he doesn't know. Completely disoriented, he tries to look at his altimeter only to find that his left hand is entangled in the ropes. He knows he is losing height and if he doesn't open his reserve parachute in time, his fall will not be broken.

Even as he is helplessly tossing in the air, another strong current luckily turns his body around again and Kadam suddenly finds his left hand free to release his emergency parachute. Using his right hand to cut away his main parachute, Kadam opens his reserve parachute. He can feel the bile in his mouth and the panic rising within but he tells himself to calm down. 'I knew that the reserve parachute is the same size as the main parachute and once that opens, my rate of descent will be the same,' he tells me, confessing that though he had started getting really worried by then, that gave him a lot of hope.

Unfortunately, there seems to be some problem with the reserve too. It should have opened in 2.5 seconds but Kadam is still falling like a rock. This time, a seriously scared Kadam realizes he is not going to fall into the Malpura dropping zone, where soil has been softened to assist in landing. He also notices that his parachute has still not opened and the ground is rushing at him at an alarming speed. Keeping incredibly calm, he does not pass out and is alert enough to remember his training.

'During all our initial jumps as we neared the landing zone, from 500 metres in the air, we could see our instructors on the ground moving around with megaphones repeatedly shouting, "Zameen nazdeek, chotta position! Zameen nazdeek, chotta position!", standard reminders that the body had to be kept compact for the fall,' he says. Even at the high speed at which he is hurtling towards the ground, Kadam automatically folds his body in the well-learned 'chotta position', bending his knees and putting his ankles together so that he hits the ground with both legs taking equal impact of the fall.

Just twenty seconds after he has jumped from the plane, Kadam smashes into the ground. He falls into a dug canal surrounded by cultivated fields along the Agra–Dholpur highway. His eyes are open, his feet are together, his reserve parachute is only half-open. He lands on top of his rucksack, which probably saves his spine, and then Kadam slowly loses consciousness.

'When I came around, I felt as if I had gone into this mystic black hole. I couldn't see a thing and I was sure it was all over for me since there seemed to be abject darkness surrounding me. And then I heard farmers. One of them lifted the parachute that had fallen on top of me and was creating the darkness and light suddenly streamed in making me blink,' he says. 'I distinctly remember one of them saying, "Arre! Yeh toh zinda hai! (He's alive!)"' Kadam just lies there with his eyes open, unable to breathe or talk—he is in complete shock. He cannot feel his body below his waist and though he can feel his upper body, he has no power to move it.

A near-comatose Kadam is picked up by the search party that has come looking for him, taken to the Air Force Station Health Centre, given tranquillizers and taken to Delhi by the same AN 32 aircraft he jumped from. Doctors find his spine intact; his knees have suffered some tendon and ligament injuries. His ankles, which took the brunt of the impact, are fractured along with the small bones of his feet—the tarsals and metatarsals. The doctors are amazed that he has survived a fall from 8,500 feet. An investigation later finds that a spring had broken during the impact tussle with the main parachute when it was not opening. This had led to a delayed opening sequence of the reserve parachute. Fortunately, it had opened partially, dulling the impact of his fall, and that is probably why Kadam lives to tell his tale.

A dream to be airborne

Kadam was eighteen when he joined the NDA. 'I had attended the Bhonsala Military School, Nashik, since I was nine years old,' he says. 'I always wanted to join the Armed Forces and wanted to be in the air.' Since medical examinations revealed a partial fusion of his L4 and L5 vertebrae, he was ruled out for the Air Force. Pilots need a sturdy spine so that in case they ever have to eject from the aircraft, the back can take the impact of the seat that will throw them in the air. Influenced by instructors in the NDA and IMA who were both paratroopers, Kadam decided to join the elite parachute regiment. That was yet another way of staying in the air, and was far more exciting too. He soon, however, realized that being a paratrooper was not as easy as he thought.

Some crazy traditions

Once he volunteered for the PARA regiment, Kadam underwent a ninety-day PARA probation course that included, amongst other things, thirty-kilometre runs carrying twenty-kilogram backpacks and weapons, socializing with officers, including some who surprised him by eating the glasses they were drinking from. Chewing on glass edges is a crazy PARA tradition that leads to ladies complaining that young officers come home for dinner and ruin their expensive sets of glasses!

After clearing the probation, officers were sent for the Para Basic Course to the Paratrooper Training School (PTS) in Agra. 'It was a four-week course which included two weeks of ground training. One of the first things we were tested for after the ground training was completed was a fear of heights,' explains Kadam.

The PTS had an interesting way of doing that. Volunteers would be asked to climb up a fifteen-metre-high platform and jump from it with a harness attached to a fan that would control their descent. Those who were afraid of heights just could not jump off that platform and were automatically rejected. Those who cleared the basic ground training were then sent for air experience.

'They would strap fourteen-kilogram parachutes to our backs and take us up in the aircraft. It would fly up to 1,250 feet with forty of us sitting along the sides. We would then be asked to walk down to the rear exit door, stand there one by one and look down while attached to a harness, and then go back to our seats,' Kadam explains. Those who could not do it were taken out of the course. Those who could were then made to do five static line jumps in the last week of training.

A king amongst men

For the jumps, the aircraft would go to a specific height. There would be a kind of traffic light inside the aircraft. When it flashed red, it meant stop, yellow meant be ready and green meant start moving. The would-be paratroopers would then walk down the ramp to the end of the plane from where they would be asked to jump one by one. An instructor would be standing there to ensure that a time gap of approximately one second was maintained between two jumps so that there was no chance of parachutes tangling with each other.

Since these were static line jumps, a twenty-foot nylon thread tied the parachute to the plane. When the paratrooper jumped out, it would break the final tie, unfurling the parachute. The training was so intensive that the paratroopers would eat, drink and sleep para jumps. 'We were taught to hit the ground with our feet together, legs joined at the knees till the ankles and slightly bent to minimize impact. A regular joke was that if a paratrooper ever falls out of bed, he will land with both feet together, knees bent,' laughs Kadam.

'Being a paratrooper is awesome,' says Kadam, 'You feel like a king amongst men.' He says he started enjoying the adrenaline rush of the jumps so much that he would volunteer for any opportunity to do one. 'If a unit was having para jumps to celebrate its raising day, or there was a command jump vacancy, I would be the first to volunteer,' he smiles. In four-and-a-half years, Kadam had completed thirty-seven static line jumps.

He then came across a free fall course that had fifteen vacancies and immediately volunteered. 'We would have Air Force instructors jumping with us with helmet-mounted cameras. They would film our jumps and later show us those videos to point out our mistakes,' Kadam recollects. The highest altitude from which Kadam jumped is 12,500 feet. 'Free fallers jump from higher than that also but they need to carry oxygen because the air becomes really thin at those heights,' he says. His twenty-sixth jump did not go too well because the strap of the rucksack attached to his thigh snapped. It hung onto only one of his legs, disturbing his balance but he managed to maintain his position and land safely. When he went for his twenty-seventh jump, the previous jump weighed on his mind. He says, 'They say your first jump is always your best because you don't worry about what can go wrong. As your air experience increases, your confidence to face any eventuality goes up.' Kadam was in the last leg of the course when the freak accident happened.

'I want the bird on my chest . . .'

It has been seven years since that fateful fall and Kadam leads a completely normal life now. He does not play games like basketball and tennis where a lot of quick ankle movements are required but he clocks nearly fifteen kilometres of cycling every day, adding an hour of swimming in the summers. 'I do my morning PT with my men, weight training and regular gym workouts. Life is perfect but for a small wish that remains to be fulfilled,' he says. 'I can go and skydive in Dubai any time I want but I want to get into shape so that I can complete the three remaining free falls that will make me a combat free-faller. I want to wear that insignia on my chest,' he says. He is working towards that goal and it will probably take him two more years. The extensive swimming and cycling is part of his agenda to build strong leg muscles. As I bid a cheerful goodbye to Kadam and his bicycle, I'm pretty sure the next time I see him, the bird shall be sitting on his chest. Some men are meant to spread their wings and fly!

11

'They were hanging between life and death when he dropped down from the sky.'

Havildar Krishna Kumar (Retd.) remembers the famous Timber Trail cable car rescue by Colonel Ivan Crasto, Shaurya Chakra, PARA (SF).

13 October 1992

A freak accident takes place in Parwanoo, Himachal Pradesh, sending the country into shock. The wire of a cable car operating between two branches of the Timber Trail Hotel, one of which is at the roadside and the other three kilometres away on the hill, snaps, bringing the car keeling down midway. There are ten tourists in the car, including four women and a child, whose lives now hang in the balance. The Army is immediately requested for help.

The story goes that a Hindu lady on that ill-fated cable car, is desperately praying to her gods for her life when an Air Force helicopter comes down from the sky. In a wonderful coincidence of national integration and religious harmony, it is being flown by Group Captain Fali Homi Major, a Parsi pilot, and has on board three PARA commandos—Major Ivan Crasto (a Goan Christian), Havildar Krishna Kumar (a Jat from Rohtak) and Havildar Joga Singh (a young Sikh). Crasto climbs down on a rope from the hovering helicopter to rescue her and nine others.

This is the story of that amazing rescue. Since Major Crasto, the hero of that rescue, who rose to become a Colonel, and has since then retired and, I was told, teaches maths to children in Australia, could not be contacted, this extraordinary story is related by Subedar Krishna Kumar (Retd.) who was a Havildar then and also on the rescue team. He has since settled down in Delhi.

A call for help

13 October 1992
Nahan, Himachal Pradesh

At the 1 PARA (Special Forces) unit there has been a small celebration. It is Havildar Krishna Kumar's thirty-eighth birthday. That morning, he has prayed to God to enable him to help as many people as he can. 'The day passed uneventfully,' he says, telling me the story of the Timber Trail operation, fourteen years after Major Ivan Crasto slithered down a rope from a helicopter and saved the lives of tourists stuck 1,155 feet above the ground in a small rope trolley.

Krishna is sixty-two now but he says every detail of that operation is stamped on his memory as if it happened yesterday. It was 8 p.m., he remembers. He had finished dinner, changed and was about to retire for the night when he heard voices carrying up from the ground floor. 'It was my Havildar Major talking to someone. He was talking about an operation in the night. I could guess something really serious had happened and was already in my combat dress by the time he reached my room.'

Krishna was hurrying down to the battalion store to withdraw his weapon when he ran into his CO Colonel (later Major General) P.C. Bhardwaj and Major (later Colonel) Crasto who were in a jonga and they stopped. 'Standing in the headlights of the jonga, CO Sahib told me that ten civilians were stuck in a cable car whose cable had broken loose in a place called Parwanoo on the Kalka–Shimla Road, and that Crasto Sahib had chosen me as his buddy for the operation.'

They told him they were driving down to the site of the accident and he should withdraw the required rescue equipment from the store and get there with a team of soldiers. Krishna picked up some rock-climbing equipment like ropes, carabiners (metal rings with a spring clip used to connect ropes), rappelling gloves and even skydiving parachutes since he had been told that the trolley was stuck at 1,155 feet. 'I had done 5,000 jumps by then and felt that if need be, we could do the rescue with parachutes on our backs so that even if we fell, we would have the option to open those,' he says.

The soldiers reached the Timber Trail Hotel at 11 p.m. The ropeway ran between two branches of the hotel, one of which was at the roadside and the other three kilometres away on the hill. The trolley wire had snapped just before it reached the other end and it had come keeling down midway where it was hanging. Krishna says they could not see anything in the dark. 'We couldn't hear anything from up there either. No one had any idea what was happening in the trolley,' he says. The CO had already decided that the operation could only be done with a helicopter in the daytime.

After waiting in the hotel for the night to pass, Crasto, Krishna and the men drove down to Chandimandir helipad at first light. A small Chetak helicopter took off from there with two pilots, Major Crasto, Colonel Bhardwaj and Havildar Krishna on board. They flew over the stuck trolley to assess the situation. 'One of the cables had broken and entwined around the other one. We didn't want to disturb the balance of the trolley in any way since we didn't know just how long it would hold,' says Krishna. The pilot tried to take the chopper down but the hilly terrain and a power line passing very close to the trolley made it very risky. The helicopter was required to hover for a long duration to effect any kind of rescue. However, the pilots said they would not be able to help since they were not trained enough and the chopper was very small. They took three rounds of the trolley and decided to return to Chandimandir.

A much larger Mi-17 chopper was called for from the Sarsawa military base and it reached Parwanoo in two-and-a-half hours. The PARA commandos were delighted since they had trained with the same chopper and one of the pilots—Group Captain F.H. Major (later Chief of Air Staff)—only a month ago. 'We had practised slithering, rappelling and other exercises on the same chopper and it brought us a lot of confidence to have it with us on this operation,' says Krishna.

In the late afternoon, the Mi-17 lifted off with Major Crasto, Havildar Krishna and a young Sikh soldier, Havildar Joga Singh, on board. The chopper made two rounds of a recce and those on board measured the risks and tried to figure out exactly how the rescue would be effected. With their plan finalized, the chopper hovered steadily over the trolley, carefully keeping itself clear of the hanging wires and electricity cables, while Major Crasto tied himself to a harness and slithered down to land on the top of the trolley. It was just about three feet in diameter.

Carefully balancing himself on the slippery top, he managed to open a small hatch, two feet in diameter, on top. 'A young boy, one of the panic-stricken tourists, immediately climbed out and started asking to be helped,' remembers Krishna, who had slithered down halfway by then. His CO told him to come back. The pilots were getting worried that the chopper might hit the cable hanging loose and crash. Krishna was asked to watch the back of the chopper while the harness was lowered for the boy who had climbed out and was now on the top of the cable car.

Crasto, who stayed back on the cable car, helped tie the young tourist to the harness and he was safely pulled into the hovering chopper. A lady and her eight-year-old child were the next to be coaxed out of the hatchet. They, too, were sent up in the same manner. By now, dusk had fallen. With lowered visibility, the pilots did not want to take the risk of an accidental crash. Crasto decided to stay back in the trolley, which was reeking of urine and excreta, to lift the morale of the scared tourists. The empty harness was withdrawn and with a parting wave from the pilots, it flew off.

Crasto spent the night with the scared tourists, cheering them up by singing songs with them and cracking jokes. 'I have a four-year-old son and wouldn't have stayed here if I didn't think it was safe,' he told them, imploring them to be brave. In reality, no one knew just how long the cable would hold and if it snapped it would plunge all of them to a painful death but Crasto kept this to himself.

The next morning, as soon as the fog lifted, the chopper was back. Huge crowds had collected on the highway by then, nearly jamming it. Everyone was watching this drama in real life unfold with bated breath. Crasto climbed out of the hatch and tying himself to the broken trolley cable, he sent the remaining tourists up to safety one by one. Each time the harness was sent down, he would tie one person to it and yank it to give them the signal to pull it up. Balancing himself on top of the narrow trolley, he managed to send all seven up.

Each time a person was sent up successfully, the crowd would break into applause. When the harness came down for the last time, Crasto strapped himself up and signalled to be pulled up. As he was taken into the chopper, a loud cheer from the crowds rent the air and a wave of pleasure across the faces of the rescued as well as the rescuers sitting in the chopper. The team got off at the helipad in Chandimandir from where the injured were sent to the hospital.

Lt Col Anupam Gaur (Retd), Army Aviation Corps, helicopter pilot

Lt Col Unnikrishnan, Para Field Company, rescued a child stuck deep inside a bore well

Col Sameer Singh Bisht, SM, Parachute Regiment, Kashmir counter-insurgency expert

Col S.S. Shekhawat, KC, SC, SM, VSM, Special Forces, most highly decorated serving officer of the Indian Army

Lt Col Satyendra Verma (Retd), Corps of Signals, skydiver and BASE jumper

Lt Col Ranveer Singh Jamwal, VSM, JAT Regiment, three-time Everest summiteer

Col Anand Swaroop, SM**, Corps of Engrs, leader of the ski expedition to the South Pole

Maj Deepika Rathore, VSM, Army Ordnance Corps, two-time Everest summiteer

Maj D.P. Singh (Retd), Dogra Regiment, Kargil war amputee and champion marathoner

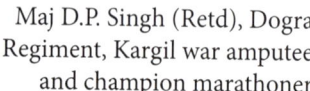

Maj Sandesh Kadam, Parachute Regiment (centre), fell from an AN 32 aircraft at 8,500 feet with an unopened parachute

Col Ivan Crasto, SC, Special Forces, hero of the Timber Trail cable car rescue

Maj Gen Ian Cardozo (Retd), AVSM, SM, Gorkha Rifles, 1971 war hero

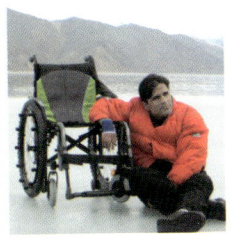

Ex Gentleman Cadet Navin Gulia, microlight pilot, adventurer and quadriplegic

Maj Raj Chaudhary, Corps of Engrs, national-level rifle shooter

Maj Shailesh Tripathi, Corps of Signals, computer expert and cyber warrior

Col Sunil Sheoran, SM, Special Forces, has been sent to 19 countries in his 25 years in uniform

Lt Manivanan P, Territorial Army, IAS and Army officer

Maj Gen S.K. Razdan (Retd), KC, Parachute Regiment, India's first general on a wheelchair

Capt Mohd Haseeb Khan, Jammu and Kashmir Light Infantry

Maj Marian Antony, Army Service Corps

Maj John Daniel, Special Forces, combat free faller, deep sea diver and jungle warfare expert

Young commissioned officers after the Passing Out Parade at the Indian Military Academy (Credit: SSB Crack)

A newly commissioned officer with his proud mother (Credit: SSB Crack)

Gentleman Cadet in his 6 Bravo Mess dress (Credit: SSB Crack)

Lady cadets undergoing strenuous training

The stately building of the Indian Military Academy, Dehradun

A Gentleman Cadet saluting

An instructor at IMA Dehradun (Credit: SSB Crack)

Pipping ceremony of Lt Col M.S. Dhoni, which he says was a childhood dream that came true when he joined the Territorial Army (Credit: ADGPI)

A young Gentleman Cadet at IMA Dehradun
(Credit: SSB Crack)

Combat forms a major part of training

The Army Adventure Cell gives young officers
opportunities to pursue adventure sports like
skydiving, mountaineering, river rafting etc.

Ascent of Mount Everest

South Pole expedition members skiing over the sastrugi, ridges formed over the snow surface by wind erosion

Freefallers jumping out of a plane

The PARA commandos got into their waiting vehicles and returned to their unit location. The news channels, newspapers and magazines continued to write about that brave rescue for a long time. But for the commandos the task was over. 'We just rested for a while and then settled back into our daily routine. We had only done our duty. That's what we were trained for,' says Krishna. Major Ivan Joseph Crasto was later awarded a Kirti Chakra for his remarkable courage and Havildar Krishna Kumar and his CO got a Shaurya Chakra each. Major Crasto, who went on to command PARA (SF), has retired and settled down in Australia. I couldn't contact him for an interview but whoever knew him says that his bravery was legendary. When I asked Subedar Krishna what kind of a man he was, he replied, 'Crasto Sahib was a hero, a real hero. Nothing could scare him. In the unit, we always knew him as a brave man—this rescue just proved it one more time.'

12

'I chopped off my leg with my own khukri.'

Major General Ian Cardozo, AVSM, SM, 4/5 Gorkha Rifles, war hero of the Indo-Pak War of 1971 relates his unbelievable story of courage and explains why he had to cut off his own foot during the '71 war.

December 1971

Deep inside what was then East Pakistan, at an airfield captured by his battalion, a young Army Major lies on the ground, stained with his own blood, gritting his teeth to bear the terrible pain he is in. His Gorkha sahayak, Rifleman Balbahadur, stands by his side, eyes wet from watching his beloved 'Cartoos' Sahib in this condition. Both of Major Ian Cardozo's legs have been badly damaged in a mine blast. The bones show through the torn flesh and muscles. His left leg is in really bad shape—a mangled foot hangs from his bloody ankle.

'Take my khukri (a Gorkha knife) and cut this damn thing off,' he orders his sahayak, his voice like steel in spite of the anguish he is in.

'Mo garnu sakdaina, Sahib,' the faithful Gorkha soldier replies. 'Doctor Sahib lai intezaar garnus.' (I will not be able to do it, sir. You'll have to wait for the doctor).

In reply, Cardozo picks up his khukri, lifts it high in the air and with a fierce slash of its blade chops off his bone a little above the ankle, separating the destroyed foot from the rest of his leg. He then tells his sahayak to go bury it outside and closes his eyes, his head dropping back wearily onto the ground.

Forty-six years later, I am on my way to the United Services Institution (USI) Library, New Delhi. I am fifteen minutes early for my appointment, eager to hear with my own ears the unbelievable story that I have read so many times in so many places. Major General Ian Cardozo (Retd.), AVSM, SM, walks in. Handsome and silver-haired, he is wearing a blue blazer with the World War I centenary poppy pinned to his lapel in remembrance of soldiers who died fighting. It signifies the legend: 'They shall not get old, as we that are left grow old.' Though the General candidly tells me that his leg muscles are weakening with age and doctors have recently detected a piece of shrapnel from the 1965 war in his skull, to me he appears pretty ageless too.

When I ask him about that act of courage still reverently remembered in Army Messes across the country even today when young officers sit down for a drink, he dismisses it with an embarrassed shrug but lets me onto a personal joke. 'I tell my wife I have a piece of land in Bangladesh—one foot by one foot, by one foot—which is my own foot.' And that balmy winter morning, sitting across the table from me in the quiet USI library, Gen Cardozo tells me his amazing story.

December 1971, Sylhet, Bangladesh

India's war with Pakistan is over. As many as 7,000 Pakistani soldiers have surrendered. Just one day after the surrender, Major Ian Cardozo of 4/5 Gorkha Rifles gets a panic call from a Border Security Force (BSF) commander near his post. He is afraid the Pakistanis might attack him. Gathering a patrol of three men, Cardozo and his Gorkhas, none of who know fear, decide to reassure him with a visit. The patrol starts walking towards the BSF location, not realizing that the Pakistanis have laid a minefield in that area.

Around 8.30 a.m., Cardozo steps on a mine. It blows up, reducing his legs to blood and bone. Much to the horror of his Gorkha troops, he falls. One of his legs is completely mangled ankle down. They carry a still conscious Cardozo back. In terrible pain, he is asking for a painkiller. 'Give me morphine,' he whispers hoarsely to the unit doctor.

The doctor reminds him that Pakistani shelling has destroyed their medical inspection (MI) room, killing one JCO, four jawans and destroying all medical stores. Cardozo tells him to cut off the leg and the doctor replies he has nothing to amputate it with and will try to organize some medication. By 10.30 a.m., Cardozo is writhing in pain and has reached the end of his patience. The destroyed foot is hurting and he can see that it will never be of any use. In desperation, he cuts it off himself.

The doctor returns and is shocked to see what Cardozo has done. 'Don't lecture me,' Cardozo tells him. 'Just tie up the leg and stop the bleeding.' The CO rushes to the location as well. By now Dhaka has fallen, the instrument of surrender is going to be signed and VIP movement has begun. All helicopters are engaged and there are none available to fly the wounded Major to an Indian Army hospital.

The Pakistanis, however, have hospitals operational in the area. Cardozo's CO tells him that they have heard about his injury and have offered to operate on him. Cardozo initially refuses. After much persuasion, he agrees on two conditions. The first is that since he doesn't trust the Pakistanis, his CO will be present while the surgery is happening to ensure that they don't touch his other leg. The second condition is that he will not accept any Pakistani blood. When his CO tells him he is being a fool, Cardozo replies, 'Sir, I'd rather die a fool than live with Pakistani blood in my veins.' After that, he blacks out. He is operated upon by Major Mohammad Bashir, who does a 'good job' but Cardozo is not able to thank him for it because he never sees him again.

Cartoos Sahib

Popularly called Cartoos (Hindi for bullet) Sahib by his brave Gorkha troops, who can't pronounce Cardozo, the Gorkhali-speaking General Cardozo was commissioned into the

1/5 Gorkha Rifles but fought two wars—1965 and 1971—with 4/5 Gorkha Rifles. He has many firsts to his name. To name a few, he was the first NDA cadet to be awarded both gold and silver medals at the Academy. He received India's first Sena Medal for gallantry when he was a twenty-three-year-old Second Lieutenant for a successful patrol he undertook in the Daporijo area of Arunachal Pradesh. He saved a raft from capsizing by jumping in the freezing water with his men and evading an attack by tribals who used bows and poisonous arrows to fight.

He is also the first disabled officer to command an infantry battalion. And the only guy most people know who cut off his own leg! That must have taken a lot of courage. So my first question for him is, 'What makes you fearless?'

'Oh no! I'm not fearless,' he quickly repartees. 'I don't think anyone is fearless—except the Gorkhas. Everyone is afraid of something. Some people are afraid of many things. What you need to do is conquer that fear.' The General managed to do that when he was a seventeen-year-old cadet in the NDA.

The cadet who didn't know how to cycle

When seventeen-year-old Ian is packing his bags to go to the NDA, his concerned parents call him in for a pep talk. His mother tells him, 'Ian, don't ever do anything that I will be ashamed of.'

His father says, 'You will command men one day. Never show fear. Fear and courage are two sides of the same coin. If you show courage, your men will follow you right into hell but if you are scared, they will not perform.'

Ian remembers and follows that advice all his life. When he reaches the Joint Services Wing at Clement Town, Dehradun (later to become the NDA and move to the Pune campus), the biggest problem he faces is that he does not know how to cycle. 'I was in Mumbai where our house was close to a busy road—I barely knew how to mount and dismount from a bicycle,' he says. The result is that he falls so many times that he ends up destroying his bicycle.

He isn't issued another one and has vivid memories of running from one class to another while all the other cadets are cycling. 'I was always running late for classes, missing breakfast, skipping dinner and being punished. In six weeks, I had lost seven kilograms and I was also at the bottom of my class,' he confesses. Studies are a big shock to him too, since he has come to the NDA under the impression that he would not have to study any more. 'I was horrified to find I had to learn science, humanities, arts besides a total of thirty-six subjects,' he says. However, his saving grace is that he was good at sports. This impressed his divisional officer who told him to sort out his maths and Hindi, assuring him that he would shoot up in the course if he did so.

Since Ian doesn't have any time during the day, he starts breaking an Academy rule. After lights out at 10 p.m., he would pull a blanket over his head and study maths and Hindi in the light of his torch. It pays off—in his fifth term, he stands second in class in the order of merit. He also starts boxing and catches the eye of his seniors because irrespective of how many beatings he takes, he never gives up. He shares an incident when he had to fight the captain of the boxing team. 'I didn't want to fight him so I reduced my weight to change my category,' the General says. However, the captain was equally keen to fight Ian so he also reduced his weight.

The entire Academy turns up to watch the fight. 'I was the Sergeant Major and nobody liked me, so they all wanted to see me get thrashed,' he says. The crowds are not disappointed. Ian does get the thrashing of his life but he digs his heels in and refuses to get knocked out. This leaves him bloody-nosed and weak-jawed but the result is that all his seniors and officers are very impressed by his grit and determination and he is made Academy Cadet Captain, a position akin to the Head Boy of the Academy.

Unfortunately, Ian rubs a British officer the wrong way by refusing to mimic an Indian officer at a battalion social. The British officer threatens him with dire circumstances, including not being allowed to lead the parade, but Ian sticks to his guns. He is in the running for one of the Academy medals. However, he is now pretty certain he is not going to get it. At the Passing Out Parade rehearsals, he notices that the gold and silver medals are both going to another cadet. This convinces him that he was not getting a medal. Imagine his surprise on D-Day when not only does he get to command the parade but when the name of the cadet receiving both medals is announced, it is none other than Academy Cadet Captain Ian Cardozo himself! 'That taught me the lesson that if you are good and if you stick to your principles, nothing can stop you,' he smiles.

The real fight

Young Cardozo's real fight, however, is to begin after the 1971 war ended. 'Because I did not have a leg, the Indian Army was not ready to give me a battalion to command,' the General explains. To prove that he is fit to command soldiers in war, he participates in the Battle Physical Efficiency Test that the Army has exempted him from because of his disability. It is a timed two-kilometre run. 'I ran the distance effortlessly, leaving seven officers with two legs behind me,' he smiles.

Another incident that helps him make his point occurs by sheer chance. Posted in the Military Operations Directorate in New Delhi, he accompanies the Vice Chief of Army Staff to Jammu and Kashmir. The Vice Chief visits the posts by chopper and Cardozo brings the convoy of vehicles by road. At one post, he decides to go and meet a course mate commanding men on top of a 4,700-foot hill. When the Vice Chief lands there, he finds Cardozo lining up to salute him, and is pretty sure that he has wrangled a helicopter ride.

'How did you reach here?' he asks curtly.

'I started at 3 a.m. and climbed up, sir,' Cardozo replies.

This impresses the Vice Chief so much that he conveys it to the Army Chief and Colonel Cardozo is sent to command 1/5 Gorkha Rifles, his first battalion.

A forty-kilometre march in the sand

Having served in 4/5 Gorkha Rifles for most of his career, Cardozo returns to his own battalion after eighteen years.

'They were in the deserts of Rajasthan and I joined them there, taking two bottles of scotch with me—only to find that no one knew me or seemed happy to see me,' he says. 'They didn't want a CO with a wooden leg who they felt would not be able to command a crack battalion.' Their new CO is about to prove them wrong.

He asks what the schedule is for the next day, only to be told that the battalion is going for a forty-kilometre march in the desert. Though he has been preparing for physical activity by doing six-kilometre runs every day, Cardozo knows very well that marching in the sand is another ball game altogether. He is offered a jeep but tells his second-in-command that he will march with the men. 'I told myself that if I cannot march with them, then I am not entitled to command this battalion,' he says. At 5 a.m. the next morning, he asks for a map, a compass and a guide—and starts walking.

The young and sturdy Gorkhas make good progress. Colonel Cardozo, who is slower since he has no ankle, follows them. When the soldiers stop to readjust their equipment after an hour, they see him coming up from behind them. He moves on, not stopping to rest. 'Budho le ke bhayo?' (What's wrong with the old man?) the men whisper to each other, wanting to know why he is not taking a break.

They are told that he has lost a leg in the 1971 war but is still keeping up with them. The fact is much appreciated. 'That day, I marched from 5 a.m. to 6 p.m.,' General Cardozo tells me. 'When I saw the end, I got a surge of confidence. I knew nothing could stop me now. In the language of the disabled, we call it empowerment. Even though I was disabled, I was as good as anybody else,' he says. After I reached, I called for the company commanders and told them, 'Gentlemen, if you think you have tested me, forget it—I have tested myself. From now on, ensure you meet *my* standards of physical fitness.'

The next physical test lined up for the battalion is a 150-kilometre route march that is to be completed in three days. 'I did that too,' says General Cardozo. After that, the CO with one wooden leg pushes the battalion till they have won every competition. He proves to them, and more importantly to himself, that he does not need two 'normal' legs to be the best possible CO. 'The lesson learnt from this is to never give up in life,' he says, smiling across the table at me.

A Boy in the Sea

Sometime after the route marches that made the Gorkhas start admiring their CO, a picnic took place at Kovalam beach when the battalion was posted in Trivandrum. 'It was June, the monsoons were about to begin, and the sea was really rough,' recounts the General. Quite suddenly, there is a cry that an officer's son has got carried away in the sea. The child keeps shouting for help but no one has the courage to jump in the wild and choppy water. Being a good swimmer, Colonel Cardozo decides to do it himself. He quickly removes his artificial leg and holding on to the shoulders of two young officers, he hops across the wet sand, making them launch him into the ocean.

Once in the water, he swims towards the drowning child, using powerful strokes to quickly cover the distance of 800 metres. 'When I reached him, the boy was panicking. I told him, "Son, don't touch me. If you cling on, we will both drown,"' General Cardozo remembers. 'I told him I would push him to the rocks and help him climb up. Someone would come to rescue him from there.'

Using all his strength, he then pushed the boy towards the rocks and made sure he had scrambled up to safety. Since Cardozo himself does not have a leg, he is not able to climb up himself. So he swims back across the tide, taking forty-five minutes to reach the beach. The incident proves to the battalion beyond any doubt that this guy means business. The tale travels to the barracks, becomes a part of langar legend and the Gorkhas are full of respect for their 'Cartoos Sa'ab'. A respect that he has won for a lifetime, not just from them but all those in the Army—and beyond—who know about him.

With that last anecdote, General Cardozo looks at his watch and tells me he needs to leave. He has an appointment that he cannot be late for. I request him to pose for a quick picture with me which he cheerfully agrees to. He is a brave man who fought for the dignity of an instructor in the academy, who fought for his country in the '71 war and who has been fighting for the rights of war-disabled soldiers nearly all his life. He walks erect and and still runs eleven kilometres in the Mumbai Marathon every year. As I watch him go, I wonder if they make men like him any more.

13

'When you have nothing to lose,
there is no fear.'

*Ex–Gentleman Cadet Navin Gulia, microlight pilot, motor car
rallyist, adventurer, motivational speaker and quadriplegic on his
extraordinary journey.*

29 April 1995
Indian Military Academy
Dehradun

Gentleman Cadet Navin Gulia was twenty-two years old
when the accident happened. A few more days and he would
have been tossing his peaked cap in the air, taking the oath of
allegiance to the Indian Army and walking out of the IMA
as a Lieutenant with two stars on his shoulder. His childhood
dream of becoming an Army officer would have come true
and he would have been standing at the doorstep of the girl

he had loved since he was fourteen. With confidence, a smile and a proposal. However, that was not to be.

On 29 April, a few days before the Passing Out Parade, Navin, who was leading the Sangro company team in the inter-company infantry obstacle crossing competition, was accidentally pushed by a teammate and fell off a ten-foot-high ramp, his lower neck taking the full impact of the fall. He would never walk again—he had been paralysed for life. And that's the condition he was in when I met him for the first time at the Military Hospital, Khadki, Pune, in the year 1996.

Navin was a fighter. He survived the three days that the doctors had given him to live after the accident. He had spent many months with a traction drilled into his head to keep his spine straight, had regained some sensation in his hands. When I met him he had just learnt to use a wheelchair and was doing a computer course at the Queen Mary's Technical Institute for Differently Abled Soldiers, near the MH. Every day, he would wheel himself 500 metres to the institute through a back gate of the hospital that was opened only for him. I was a reporter on the health beat at the *Indian Express* looking for new stories every day. He first became a story and then a friend.

Bud dy, with a space in between

August 2016
Air Force Station, Palam, Delhi Cantonment

I'm on a post-dinner stroll outside my house when the Dev Anand ditty playing on my earphones is interrupted by a text notification. A message flashes on my cell screen: 'Hi bud dy, can I call?'

It's Navin. That's how he has started spelling buddy lately—bud dy, with a space in between—since both of us have gotten busy with our lives and don't have much time for each other any more. I immediately call back and find him really excited about a new mouth organ he has bought.

'I'm still getting used to it but I can play you a song,' he offers. And as I walk under the trees in the moonlight, a tune rings out in my ears. It's a little off-key and I worry a bit because I won't be able to identify it if he asks me to but luckily, he doesn't. He is planning a picnic to Bhardwaj Lake that he has recently discovered in the Asola-Bhatti Wildlife Sanctuary between Gurgaon and Faridabad. 'It's got brilliant blue water like the Pangong Tso. It's just forty kilometres from here but we'll need a four-wheel drive to get there. I can take my jeep,' he says.

Well, that's Navin, my bud dy with a space in between—a space that we're trying to bridge. What most people notice first about Navin is that he is a quadriplegic but now that I've known him for years, I don't even register that he moves around in a wheelchair—except when he knocks down my favourite pot trying to manoeuvre the wheelchair through my narrow sitting room door.

Usually accompanied by his effervescent wife Khushi and a noisy, yelping pug called Champu Chamgadar that they have recently acquired, Navin is full of life—ready to help, guide, crack jokes, treat you to momos or participate in a samosa-devouring round. His enthusiasm levels have not come down a single notch from when he would go around Pune's Khadki Military Hospital pushing his wheelchair inch by painful inch with a stern 'Do Not Push' that he had got someone to write behind it with red paint.

Remind him of those times and he chuckles and says that it was so exasperating when people (no doubt with the best intentions), sometimes perfect strangers, would push him around the hospital, pitying his slow progress. What they didn't understand was that he was only trying to do it on his own to exercise his hands. 'Sometimes I would take thirty minutes to get down a ramp (in a wheelchair, it has to done backwards since you arrive before your wheelchair if you do it the other way) and just when I was ready to celebrate my descent, someone would push me up again, thinking I was trying to go up.'

A relentless determination

The first time I saw Navin, he was trying to get used to the spinal injury that had transformed his life completely. On that rain-soaked Pune afternoon, when I didn't know what to say to a young man whose career and life had come crashing down because of a freak accident, he made things comfortable for me. He was cracking a joke with a nurse and laughing loudly when he turned to include me in the warmth of his smile. At the time, he was also fighting with the government to grant him officer status and a pension since he had got injured on the last day of his course at the IMA.

I decided to write an article about it and we combed through his papers and the Army rules to get the facts right. Though it looked unlikely to me that he would get what he wanted, I still wrote that piece because he was so confident about getting his due. Not only did the pension come to him but I've watched him get almost everything that he has aspired to since then.

'People say disability slows life down for a person but I feel it helps you do things sooner. You develop the mindset "ke jo bhi karna hai, abhi karna hai (whatever needs to be done, has to be done right now.)". Look at the things I have managed to achieve since I became disabled. Had I been fine, it would have probably taken me twice as long to do any of these!' Navin says. 'I even wrote my autobiography in 2011 at the age of thirty-eight,' he smiles.

Life after the accident

Calling Navin a role model for the differently abled does not do him enough justice. He is a role model to all of us who have dreams that we don't always have the courage to pursue and who are restricted by our own acceptance of our limitations. He is a living example of his favourite saying, 'Our ability never restricts us, our thoughts do. If we think we can, we can.'

Navin regrets that the cadet who pushed him never came to meet him after the accident. 'I would have liked to tell him not to let it weigh on his mind because accidents happen. But he could probably never face me because of the guilt,' he tells me. He says he never thought about who had pushed him because it did not matter. But he thought a lot about how he could still get on with all the things he wanted to do.

Flashback to April 1995
Dehradun

When a shocked Navin, in excruciating pain and no longer able to feel his body, is brought to the Dehradun Military Hospital, doctors realize that his spinal cord has broken and his body is paralysed, most likely forever. A traction is screwed into his head to keep it completely still and the doctors give him three days. If he survives those, he has a better chance to live. Not only does Navin pull through those days, he goes on to do things that a person with legs or even wings would have found difficult. His is a story of unbelievable, inspiring courage, both mental and physical, for which had he still been in the Army, he would have probably got a chestful of medals.

Navin spends many months lying on his hospital bed in traction. He says he spent that time looking at a spider weaving a web above him on the ceiling, while making a mental list of all the things he would never be able to do. 'I would never be an Army officer, I would not be able to write, I would not be able to use my limbs . . . the list was endless. But then I taught myself to be proud of what I had. I started finding ways to make myself worthy of that pride,' he says. 'I can never understand the concept of giving up. You would have to have really low self-esteem for that,' he says. 'And I don't.'

So Navin hangs a book from his hospital bed and starts to read, he practises mental chess on an empty chessboard; and after a two-year stint recovering in the hospital, he studies for and passes a computer proficiency course at Aptech with 99 per cent marks. He has his friends carry him up the forty stairs of the Symbiosis Institute every day and completes his master's degree in computer management with first class marks. He starts teaching maths and computer science for a living, and fights to obtain a driving licence. When car manufacturers do not show any interest in his hand-control designs, he goes ahead to design a hand-driving kit for the differently abled that can be attached to any car.

'The best way to empower a person is to take everything away from him. When you have nothing to lose, there is no fear,' Navin says with a smile. Who would know this better than him? When the doctors pronounced him 100 per cent disabled, Navin challenged those limitations, and strove relentlessly to achieve whatever targets he set for himself. Despite limited sensation below his shoulders, he has taught himself to drive cars and motorized gliders. 'With practice you can do anything,' he says. 'And I was never afraid of hard work.'

He has designed controls that let him handle an automobile's clutch, brake and accelerator simultaneously and uses them by pushing his arm, by moving his shoulder. 'Flying is easier than driving. The controls are so much less complicated. Pull the steering and the plane goes up, push it down and it comes down. Unlike a car, a plane cannot topple. So I found flying even easier than driving,' he explains.

Finding love and purpose

His zest for life has worked on the romance front too. He found his dream girl Khushi, a Goan, on a forum online and she was so enamoured with him that she dropped everything and came to Delhi to marry him.

Navin started on his adventures by setting a Limca World Record for driving a Tata Safari to Marsimik La, the highest mountain pass in the world. At 18,632 feet, as the milestone there proclaims, it is 1,232 feet higher than the Everest Base Camp (17,400 feet). Navin has an interesting story linked to this achievement and I chuckle heartily when I hear it. When Navin was in the Academy, he would write every day to the girl he had been in love with from his school days in Meerut. However, after a while he stopped receiving any letters from her. He planned to visit her after he got his commission but that was not to be.

Soon after his accident, he was moved to Delhi for treatment, and was surprised by a visit from her as she had heard about his injury from a common friend. She was now married and came to see him with her husband. Navin then realized that her parents kept his letters from her and had convinced her to get married. She was heartbroken and guilt-ridden to find him on a hospital bed. Navin convinced her to go home and promised her that he would get better soon and would let her know when he did.

Since those were the days of snail mail and Facebook did not exist, the two of them lost touch again. After he got better, Navin had no way of communicating with her. 'Since

I had promised her I would let her know I was fine, I decided that if I became famous by some means, she would also get to hear of it. And that,' he says, laughing heartily, 'was one of my major reasons for undertaking an expedition that would create a world record.' She did see him on the Zee News Channel when his world record was covered by the media and got in touch with him, relieved that he had recovered. 'We are still friends,' Navin says. 'Both of us are happy in our own worlds.'

Spreading joy

Navin has spread that happiness through every sphere of his life and to everyone that he has come in contact with. He has modified cars for polio-affected people, designed controls for the differently-abled, given motivational talks to soldiers disabled by war and insurgency, toured hospitals to share his infectious enthusiasm and will to live a happy life with other veterans wounded in war and paraplegics.

He has also held the position of senior coordinator at the War Wounded Foundation in New Delhi, and now runs two NGOs—Apni Duniya Apna Ashiana (ADAA) and Jan Jagriti—in Delhi that work with street and rural children. In 2005, he adopted Barhana, a village in Haryana that has one of the lowest male–female ratios in the country. 'They have 376 girls to 1000 boys. We are trying to support girls in the village and help them build successful lives so that they are a motivation to other girls and to their parents,' he explains.

The sales for his autobiography, *In Quest of the Last Victory*, have touched one lakh copies already. His efforts to inspire and lead have been recognized and he has received the Chief of Army Staff commendation for exemplary service in 2005 and the National Role Model Award from former President A.P.J. Abdul Kalam in 2006. Navin is a busy man now. He doesn't come home as often as I would like him to. Yet, when he does drop in with his lovely family, his effervescent wife Khushi, Saroj, his teenage boy Friday, and Champu the pug, deftly manoeuvring his customized olive-green jeep into the driveway of my house, the years in between just disappear. He comes across as the same twenty-three-year-old I first met in Pune, who went around his wheelchair with a red 'Do Not Push" written behind it. Though I just roll my eyes in mock exasperation when he starts irritating me and Khushi with just how awesome, how good-looking, how unbelievably wonderful he is, it's actually all true. He is one of the most amazing guys I know. And whenever I think about it, my heart fills with admiration for the long and arduous journey he has made.

This piece has appeared in *www.yourstory.com.*

Training to be a Soldier

How do they turn long-haired kids into superheroes who can shoot at a moving target and ballroom dance with the same élan *that they can ride a horse? Or, how do you earn work clothes that will completely floor the opposite sex?*

14

'At twenty-five, you will lead a 100 men ready to die at your command.'

Lieutenant Mohammad Haseeb Khan, Jammu and Kashmir Light Infantry, talks about his journey from a long-haired college kid to a lean, mean fighting machine.

A day at the Academy

Fit and confident, with warm eyes and a sparkling smile, twenty-two-year-old Lieutenant Mohammad Haseeb Khan talks to me while doing the Young Officers course in Mhow to tell me about the training every Army officer has to undergo. 'I have an hour,' he says, looking at his watch, and starts by sharing with me his most vivid childhood memory.

'We used to live in the Lucknow cantonment. It was my fourth birthday, or maybe fifth,' he says, nostalgically. 'My father, Naib Subedar Mohammad Saleem Khan, screened the movie *Border* for all my friends. He placed a TV on the ground outside our house and all of us sat there, open-mouthed, watching Sunny Deol play Major Kuldip Singh Chandpuri, the famous hero of the Battle of Longewala in 1971. For many days after that, we would go around with sticks balanced on our shoulders, pretending they were guns,' he laughs. 'I think that was my first inspiration to join the Army.' However, Khan was destined for greater things. He joined the paltan of the famed Param Vir Chakra awardee, Subedar Major and Honorary Captain Bana Singh, PVC, after whom a post at the Siachen Glacier is also named.

The Khans were living in Sector 14 in Dwarka, New Delhi, when the call came from the OTA in Chennai. In October 2014, he boarded a train for Chennai, embarking on a three-day journey that would take him there. Khan says as soon he was granted admission to the OTA, he had started running and going to the gym to prepare for the physical rigour of the Academy. 'But nothing prepares you for what's actually in store for you,' he smiles.

Gentleman Cadet at nineteen

An OTA bus comes to pick up the fifty young boys who are waiting nervously at the Chennai railway station. They have come from all parts of the country—from Bengaluru to Bengal—and don't know each other yet. But in one year, they will turn into friends for life who will not only be ready to live but also die for each other. The OTA has seven companies (five for Gentlemen Cadets (GCs) and two for Lady Cadets (LCs) and each cadet is allotted one. Gentleman Cadet Khan gets assigned to Naushera. Around 1 p.m., he is standing outside the company block with forty-nine others.

The seniors step out and welcome them to the Academy. They say the boys will have to prove they are worthy of Naushera. To do this is quick and easy. 'Nine knuckle push-ups on the road and you can come in,' a stern-faced senior tells them, stifling a smile. One by one, all fifty do the required push-ups, some more easily than others, and are allowed to pick up their luggage and come inside the building. Khan says he found it tough but managed to do all nine.

Once inside, each cadet becomes an understudy to a senior cadet who will be their friend, philosopher and guide during their months at the OTA. Khan is understudy to Gentleman Cadet Anuj Kumar. 'Over the months, he guided me with everything—right from fixing my uniform to table manners to physical training (PT),' says Khan. When I couldn't clear my PT test, he would call me to his room and make me practise. It was a great support system to have him around,' he says.

The first one month at the Academy is called the 'honeymoon period'. Mistakes are forgiven with a reprimand, serious punishments are not given and GCs are given time to learn the ropes. Thereafter, all hell breaks loose. A tsunami of punishments awaits them if any rules are broken. If they have been given five minutes to report for a task or duty and are late by even a few seconds, they are told to bend down and start doing front rolls. Staying late at breakfast could call for twenty push-ups. If their room is found untidy during study hour, they had better be ready to run around the block a few times. A sacred drill followed religiously in both the IMA as well as the OTA is the Patti Parade.

All Army officers have very fond memories of this. When it is happening, of course, it is a frustrating race against time. The GCs have to be faster than, or at least as fast as, Clark Kent changing into his Superman costume at the revolving door. All fifty from a course are lined up and given three to four minutes, to run to their rooms and change into a specified rig. It could start with combat which means GCs have to return in the specified time wearing their combat uniform along with the cap, belt, direct moulded sole (DMS) boots and socks. They all need to be dressed and lined up before the three minutes are up.

They are then immediately sent back to change into their, for example, PT rig in the next three minutes. This means white shorts, white T-shirt, white socks and white shoes. The moment they line up, they could be ordered to change into muftis, civilian clothes for outings, encompassing a white shirt, black trousers for juniors and grey for seniors, the OTA tie and black brogue shoes. No sooner have they lined up in mufti, orders might be passed to change into their games rig which means the company colour T-shirt (red for Naushera), matching socks, black shorts and white shoes. A single person arriving late means the entire course will be punished.

'Though it was very annoying, because the entire course would be punished for a single person, it also taught us to do things together and to help the ones who were slow or facing problems. It taught us how to be a team.' This is just one of the Academy's ways of inculcating in cadets the spirit of comradeship and brotherhood of the brave. Army officers are taught to live by the motto 'One for all and all for one!' It holds great importance in operations where lives are at risk and is also a great way to live life.

On a lighter note, Khan tells me that the Patti Parade made him realize just how much his wardrobe had suddenly grown. 'From four pairs of jeans, four shirts and two pairs of shoes when I was in college, I suddenly had twenty-five shirts, twenty-five trousers and eight pairs of shoes. We would even keep an extra pair of shoes of each kind handy just in case something broke because not being in proper uniform is considered an unpardonable sin,' he says.

A daily routine

The GCs wake up around 3.30 a.m., SSB (shit, shave and brush) and collect outside in their PT dress. Tea, coffee and biscuits are then served. While seniors stand around in the corridor and have it, freshers are supposed to take their refreshments inside their rooms. At 4.30 a.m., a report is taken by one of the seniors. This is followed by instructions for the day. Those who have erred are allotted punishments. Punishable offences could include forgetting to wish a senior, slacking with table manners or not moving around the campus in a bicycle squad of four. The last one is an interesting rule that both the IMA as well as the OTA follow. GCs have to move around in groups of not less than four. If they are even one less, they have to dismount from their cycles and push them running.

All formalities are completed by 5.30 a.m., and GCs stand in a U-shape for the morning muster. One of the juniors comes up and recites the company pledge, 'We will fight for the company; we will win for the company; we have to bring back what was always ours!' (meaning, the championship banner) The pledge ends with the company war cry, 'Shera! Shera! Naushera!' The juniors then go for PT and the seniors for drill. After an hour of outdoor activity, with a twenty-minute interval in between, all GCs return to their rooms, change and fall in for breakfast which is served between 8.00 and 8.40 a.m.

As juniors, GCs get just about five minutes to eat the lavish breakfast spread. 'If we were wearing combats for an outdoor class, we would quickly swallow the omelette and drink up the milk, while stuffing our pockets with slices of bread to be devoured later in the day in between training,' shares Khan. He recounts an episode when he was punished for disobeying orders.

'It was my second week at the Academy. I was really hungry and digging into breakfast when a senior came and announced that a lecture had been preponed and we needed to clear out of the Mess in two minutes. I had kept a juicy piece of chicken aside to eat later when my senior told me to leave. "I'm leaving, Sir," I said and kept eating. He said it one more time and I gave him the same reply, while trying to finish my chicken that I just didn't have the heart to leave. He told me to come to his room at 9 a.m. the next morning,' Khan says sheepishly. Not only did GC Khan get a good firing, he also had to do forty push-ups in sets of ten. He was quite upset but another senior with a kinder heart called him to his room, gave him a pep talk and offered him a soft drink and biscuits that cheered up Khan considerably.

Class routine

Life at the Academy follows a strict and well-structured academic routine. Lectures begin at 9 a.m. Subjects taught at the Academy include English, military history, computers, science and warfare technology, weapon training and firing. On most mornings, four lectures are scheduled with a break from 10.30 a.m. to 10.50 a.m. Around 1.20 p.m., GCs break off for lunch. By 2 p.m., they return to their company, change into company colours and withdraw weapons, if required, for a class. From 3 to 4 p.m., GCs are issued uniforms, given time to visit the bank, give their cycles for repair and other chores. From 4.30 to 5.50 p.m., they play some troop games, including sports like basketball, volleyball and hockey, which all of them have to participare in and learn. They will later play these with soldiers and this helps in forming bonds so strong that men are ready to face death for each other. 'Games helped us in building relationships, taught us team spirit and cooperation, and we learnt how to cover for each other,' says Khan.

After they get back to campus, the GCs are served tea and biscuits. They are then given time to freshen up and change into muftis. From 6.45 to 7.45 p.m. is the study period when they have to be at their desks for self-study. From there, they go to the anteroom to watch some TV, play snooker or go through newspapers and journals. At 8 p.m., one of the juniors comes up and reads out the news, followed by an inspirational thought or quote, and orders are also read out for the next day. At 8.10 p.m., all of them march to the Cadet Mess for dinner.

A parade dreaded by all GCs is the Saturday evening roll call. 'That was the time when the names of all those officially being allotted punishments for serious mistakes made during the week were announced,' says Khan. 'Faces would fall for the unlucky ones. It meant they would not be able to go out on Sunday. But it was also taken with a pinch of salt.'

Super or scary Sundays

As freshers, the GCs live in mortal fear of Sundays. This is the day seniors are free to rag and punish them. But when they became seniors, Sunday became a fun day for Khan and his course mates. Today, the Academy allows GCs to keep basic phones but in 2014, when Khan did his training, phones were prohibited. So an important part of their Sunday ritual was to go to the STD booth and call home, friends and girlfriends (if you were lucky enough to have one!). 'We would get up by 6 a.m., which was pretty late by Academy standards, go for a run, PT, games and return to our blocks by 8 a.m.,' Khan says. After getting dressed, the GCs do their errands. Someone has a broken cycle to fix, someone else needs soap, toothpaste or shaving cream from the canteen. Another one might need to get a haircut, and yet another may need a nameplate or a beret. So everyone is busy getting these things together but by 11 a.m., which is brunch time, they are all back in the Mess.

A lavish brunch consisting of chole bhature, biryani or dosas is served. Only those who have cleared the drill square test, a test of saluting, marching, giving commands in the parade (that has to be cleared in the fifth–sixth week at the Academy), are allowed to dress up smartly in their muftis, making sure their OTA ties are neatly knotted, and go on liberty, which is the GCs' day out. 'We would catch some public transport and visit the malls, window shop or have a burger or pizza,' Khan says. Pubs are strictly out of bounds. All GCs have to be back by 4 p.m. They then sit together outside their block cracking jokes and singing songs or mimicking each other. At 6 p.m., a film is screened in the auditorium. Sundays are dedicated to Bollywood and Wednesdays to Hollywood films. Most of these are new releases and sometimes, they are war and action films. Attendance is compulsory for the sleep-deprived GCs who would prefer a nap to a film. However, what makes it better are the snacks and drinks—samosas, rolls and milkshakes—that are dished out in the interval by the stalls put up outside.

Unity in diversity

The Academy is a beautiful melting pot of India's various religions and regions. Khan is a roti-eating Muslim from north India, his buddy at the Academy is GC Takehel Mayun Napoleon, a rice-loving Christian from Manipur, where the definition of meat includes frogs and dogs. During the first term, freshers are discouraged from eating rice since they have to stay really slim and pass their drill test. 'While it didn't make much of difference to the rest of us, we would sneak in rice for Takehel who just couldn't eat rotis,' remembers Khan.

Another course mate, GC Gowtham R. is a Tamilian who cannot understand a word of Hindi. 'Every time an order was passed in Hindi, all of us would run around trying to implement it while Gowtham and Takehel would desperately look around for someone to translate it into English,' remembers Khan. 'While the rest of us would be learning to speak English, they had to be taught Hindi. Now Gowtham is posted to a unit in Bihar and not only does he speak flawless Hindi, he knows all the swear words there are to learn and is also WhatsApping us in Hindi all the time,' Khan laughs. 'The Academy brings you so close to your course mates that they become your friends for life. You might rise to become a General but a course mate, regardless of his rank, can walk in unannounced, abuse you wholeheartedly, pick up food from your plate and you won't say a word,' he says emotionally.

At twenty-five, you command 100 men

Khan says it was his dream to be an Army officer and this has now come true for him. In spite of being an engineering student, he preferred to join the infantry because he wanted to be a ground soldier, the first line of defence to be sent to fight a war. Khan's message to those considering a career in the Army is this: 'If you are looking for a government job with a cool lifestyle, a smart uniform and an attractive pay package but are afraid of risking your life for your country, look elsewhere. As an officer in the Indian Army, you will be responsible for the security of your country and for many other lives. At the age of twenty-five, you will be commanding 100 men who will be ready to fight and even die at your command. Don't think of this as just another career. The primary job of the Army is to fight battles and protect the nation. All those who sign up should be ready to do that.'

15

'I play troop games like football; I can shoot from a rifle and I know unarmed combat—every lady officer does.'

Major Marian Antony, Army Service Corps, on how her training ensures that she can handle a fascinating variety of things, right from unarmed combat to rifle shooting to leading a convoy and editing a magazine.

I meet Major Marian Antony on my frequent trips to South Block in the course of writing this book. She in on the Additional Directorate General of Public Information team that is helping me identify officers to be interviewed, organizing outstation visits and putting me in touch with the ones posted at undisclosed locations, often with no cell phone connectivity. Smartly dressed in her olive-green uniform, Marian is no different from a gentleman officer—accomplished, efficient and with that old world courtesy seldom seen beyond the Army. We are about to wind up the book when I feel she needs to be in it too, if only to give an idea about the fascinating variety of jobs lady officers handle in the Army. When I mention this to her, she is quite embarrassed but the necessary permission comes through and finally, we sit down to talk, this time not about things that I need help with on the book but about her own journey as a lady officer. This is Marian's story.

Slim and pretty, with a gentle smile and a polite demeanour, Major Marian Antony is the perfect example of the adage 'Looks can be deceptive'. Meet her when she's in her civvies—which could be a Kanjeevaram sari if she's going for a wedding or jeans and a casual T-shirt if she's going to a mall—and you would find it hard to believe that she can shoot to kill and use unarmed combat if required.

'Every Army officer knows how to handle a rifle and we are all taught attack and defence,' she says, smiling that gentle smile that completely belies how tough she really is.

It takes a little while but you soon get used to the fact that she will be standing up when you enter her office and opening doors for you. She is an officer of the Indian Army and follows the same rules of chivalrous behaviour that the gentlemen officers do.

Marian joined the Army as a twenty-two-year-old, fascinated by a career in uniform after life in civil society. 'Nobody from our family had ever been in the forces. My father was a hotelier in Italy and my mother was working in Dubai. Till Class XII, I couldn't have imagined being an

Army officer but I was exposed to the Army life and way of thinking when I opted for the NCC in college,' she says.

As an NCC cadet at Stella Maris College in Chennai, Marian represented Tamil Nadu at the Republic Day parade in Delhi. A good student, she hadn't really thought of a career in uniform in her college days. When she was selected both by HSBC and Accenture during the campus recruitments, she decided to join Accenture. However, after a year and a half of working there, she met an NCC senior who had joined the Army and was convinced that the Army offered some interesting opportunities. 'I decided to appear for the SSB entrance exam at her prodding since she was really enjoying being an Army officer,' Marian says. Having cleared the SSB, she joined the OTA in Chennai under the Women Special Entry Scheme.

She says she had fond memories of life as a Lady Cadet. For six months, her day began at 5 a.m. with one hour of PT followed by non-stop classes and physical activity through the day till the time they were allowed to hit their beds. 'It was tough,' she says. 'We were on the move all the time. We would barely get four hours to sleep on weekdays.' The high point of the training was the twenty-five-kilometre Josh Run that the LCs had to complete carrying ten-kilogram backpacks and rifles. This distance has now been increased to forty kilometres.

Soon after she passed out from the OTA, in March 2008, Antony got posted to Jammu and Kashmir. 'I had opted for the Army Service Corps (ASC),' she says. 'Our job is to handle the logistic support of the Army by providing rations, vehicles and other items.' In her first posting, she frequently went as convoy commander with soldiers, leading thirty to forty vehicles at a time and being responsible for their movement from one place to another. 'I would be the only lady and we would have convoys moving through the day but I never faced any problems,' she says.

In 2009, in a posting to Riyasi in Jammu and Kashmir, Marian handled an appointment at Talwana about five kilometres away, where she was the only lady officer on location and was constantly surrounded by troops. 'I was proud of the fact that my CO had faith in my capabilities to handle that appointment,' she says. Marian was responsible for the provision of dry and fresh rations as well as fuel, oil and lubricants (FOL) to the troops in the area. 'People have a lot of apprehensions about lady officers being alone at locations with troops but believe me, I have never felt safer,' she says. She agrees though that as a lady officer she had to initially prove herself to the soldiers, most of whom come from villages. 'Reporting to a woman and having her in charge was totally new to them since they had only seen women as wives or mothers, never as professionals,' she admits. 'You have to work hard to gain their trust. ASC is mostly about accounts, documentation, doing contracts and dealing with people; and if you know your job, they realize you are as good as a gentleman officer and quickly adjust.' Marian says playing troop games like volleyball and basketball with the men helps in bonding as does officer-like behaviour and not taking liberties for being a woman. 'Lady officers are now there in almost all appointments and slowly these apprehensions will go,' she says.

According to Marian, the most fascinating thing about being in the Army is that there is no monotony. During every tenure, you are doing something different. 'I have led convoys in Jammu and Kashmir, handled supply of rations to troops, worked with the Composite Food Laboratory, in Mumbai, gathering food samples of edibles like coffee powder and cashews from all over the country,' says Marian. Currently, she is posted to Delhi and works as the editor of an Army magazine, where she handles both content and design. She also provides content support and clearance of images at the Public Information office of the Army.

She has worn many hats over the course of her life but she says the Army beret has been the most interesting of them all. 'I have seen both civilian life and life in uniform. With the Army, I have had the opportunity to see almost the entire country and do a fascinating variety of jobs. I'm pretty sure a career in the civil world would have never given me that exposure,' she says, reaching out for the ringing phone. 'Yes Sir! I'll handle that, Sir,' she says; and giving me an apologetic smile, asks me if she can be excused. I assure her I have got all that I want and get up to go, leaving her to move on to her next job.

Joining the Army as a lady officer

Women have been in combat roles in the army since 1992 but they have been part of the Armed Forces Medical College since the 1960s. Presently, the tenure of lady officers in the Army is of ten years with an extension of another four years, which is called a Short Service Commission. Subject to vacancies, requirements and their performance, lady officers can be taken for a permanent commission.

Women's entry schemes

UPSC Entry: Women candidates of between nineteen to twenty-five years of age can apply for a written exam held by the UPSC twice in a year. Successful candidates are called for the SSB interview. To apply, you need to be a graduate or a postgraduate in any discipline from a recognized university.

NCC Special Entry: NCC women cadets who have two years of service in the NCC senior division Army and have a minimum B grade in C certificate exam can apply for this. Women cadets need to be between nineteen to twenty-five years old. Vacancies per course are notified by the Additional Directorate General of Recruiting. Final-year students and graduates with 50 per cent aggregate marks are eligible for this entry.

SSC-Technical Entry: Women engineering students of between twenty to twenty-seven years of age are eligible for this entry. They can apply for it while in the final year of their engineering degree or after completing their degree. A graduate in any discipline of engineering is eligible to apply.

Judge Advocate General (JAG) entry: This entry is especially for law graduates. The age required for this entry is twenty-one to twenty-seven years, which is notified along with the vacancies by the Additional Directorate General of Recruiting in the month of April or October of each year. To be eligible for this entry, a candidate must have a LLB or LLM degree with minimum 55 per cent aggregate marks and should be registered with the Bar Council of India.

16

'I stood in the snake pit watching the cobra come closer.'

Major John Daniel, PARA (Special Forces), combat free faller, deep-sea diver, jungle warfare expert talks about training and life in the Special Forces.

Locating Major John Daniel of PARA (Special Forces) for an interview is not easy. He is never in one place for long. By the time I find his parent unit location in the North-east, he has moved to Delhi. By the time I manage to get his Delhi number, he is in Kashmir. He constantly moves in and out of mobile phone coverage, never being able to answer my calls. When I finally get to him, he apologizes politely and tells me he has been busy in operations. 'We are moving around in the jungles chasing militants, Ma'am,' he says, 'There is a lot of movement across the LOC these days.'

Those who join the Special Forces live on the edge. They like to call it real soldiering. 'We take the extra risk,' says Daniel, when I can finally speak to him over intermittent conversations stretched over three days because he is on an operation in Kashmir and in and out of the jungles. The force behind these tough-as-nails men who put their lives on the line to handle some of the most difficult assignments in the country is their training. So here's a look at what it encompasses.

The Special Forces probation

December 2009
Rowriah, Jorhat

Captain John Daniel, twenty-six, stands quiet and upright in the snake pit, broom in hand, closely watching the black cobra that is slithering in his direction. It is at least five feet long. Daniel holds his breath, never taking his eyes off the cobra. Around him are more than half a dozen different snakes. He knows most of them are non-poisonous rat snakes and water snakes; the maximum damage they can do is bite him. What he has to watch out for are the three poisonous ones—the banded krait that he has recognized from the yellow and black bands on its body, the viper with the quick lashing movement of the tail and the cobra heading in his direction.

In the cold Assam winter, Daniel feels sweat on his brow. In his shirt pocket, the non-PARA volunteer form crackles as he takes a deep breath. He knows he only has to say he doesn't want to join the Special Forces and they will pull him out of the pit. He toys with the idea for a split second and then dismisses it. Taking another breath he takes a step to the side, bends down to pick the cobra by its tail and flings it away even as it hisses its disapproval. His instructor, watching from above the ten-foot-deep pit with a snake-handling tong in his hand, rewards him with a 'Shabash!'

Being dropped into the snake pit with a broom and being told to clean it is a drill almost all PARA (SF) officers are familiar with. They have all done it at least a few times. 'We are taught to identify snakes and handle them. Then, as a test, we are put in the three metre-by-two-metre pit with them. It is a test of mental toughness,' says Daniel with a nostalgic smile, remembering those days of probation.

A training that nearly kills

There are eight Special Forces units in the Indian Army, spread out from Kashmir to the North-east. Counted as amongst the deadliest in the world, these units are perpetually in the midst of action. Officers who volunteer to join have to undergo one of the toughest probations in the world. Any Army officer can volunteer for the Special Forces, whether he is a fresh graduate from the IMA in Dehradun, the OTA in Chennai or serving in any infantry unit. All volunteers have to pick any three out of the eight Special Forces units in the country. They are then called to one of the units of their choice for a probation designed to push them to the limits of their mental and physical endurance.

Besides other things, training includes long-distance swimming, endurance runs of forty kilometres carrying forty-kilogram backpacks, being thrown in the water with arms and legs tied and bouts in the snake pit. Those who last ninety days and manage to impress their instructors earn the most coveted badge in the Indian Army. The standards are so exacting that only five out of 100 officers who volunteer actually get to wear the Special Forces badge. Inspired by the British Special Forces insignia 'He who dares, wins', the Indian Special forces have the word 'Balidaan', sacrifice, written on their badge.

Every Special Forces man is a trained paratrooper and a trained swimmer. Right from dealing with insurgency to hostage crises and military surgical strikes, they are trained for all eventualities. Men are taught combat free falls of 25,000 feet where they jump with oxygen masks and cylinders, deep-sea diving, sniping, firing, unarmed combat among other skills. They are specially trained in mountain warfare because most future battles are going to be fought in the mountains.

The men are also culturally and linguistically trained so that they can operate in other countries. They speak languages like Pashto, Arabic, Chinese, Tibetan, which are taught to them in the Education School at Panchmari and the School of Foreign Languages in Delhi. Special Forces volunteers are bluntly told that they have to be much tougher than the average soldier. While an infantry soldier does forty minutes of PT, in the Special Forces they do one and half hours. While infantry men do hand push-ups, Special Forces men do knuckle push-ups. While an infantry soldier fights with weapons, Special Forces soldiers are taught to fight without weapons. Normal soldiers are trained for land attacks, Special Forces units are trained to attack from the sea and the air too.

Daniel's story

Daniel says he was influenced to join the Army by his father Havildar P.G. Daniel, who served in the Corps of Electronics and Mechanical Engineers (EME) and also his student days in Army Public School, Noida. 'I studied there from Class VIII to XII. Out of the twenty-five boys in my class, twelve joined the Armed Forces. It was a dream so many of us had and we constantly talked about it and pushed each other to do it,' he says. Daniel could not make it to the NDA merit list and opted to do law from the Army Institute of Law at Mohali. He got through his CDS exam thereafter and in July 2005, he went to the IMA. 'I had got selected for the Air Force too but the Army was my first choice,' he says.

He was twenty-two years old when he graduated from the IMA. He joined 2 Ladakh Scouts, which works primarily in Siachen and Ladakh. Daniel says he was inspired to join the Special Forces by an instructor in the Academy who was from the Special Forces and later by his unit second-in-command Major Vivek Jasrotia from PARA (Special Forces). 'He was a Commando Dagger (the best in his commando course) and had seen a lot of action. Most of us looked upon him as a role model and we were completely awestruck by his stories from the North-east and Jammu and Kashmir,' he says. 'I started believing that real soldiering was in the Special Forces and decided to volunteer. My choice was naturally PARA (Special Forces).' Married two years back, Daniel says he is lucky to have found a partner who understands his passion for the Special Forces. 'In the last one year, we could only spend twenty days together, that too after a gap of more than eleven months,' he says. 'It is not easy being in the Special Forces but that is what I want to do.'

Daniel's probation

December 2009

It is 1 a.m. when the New Delhi Rajdhani Express winds into Mariani railway station in Assam with a shudder and a sigh. In the quietness of the night, a slim, young officer with a crew cut, wearing jeans and a thick jacket jumps out of the second AC coach, pulling out a black steel box after him. It is twenty-six-year-old Captain John Daniel reporting to PARA (SF) for his Special Services probation. Daniel is coming straight from Siachen where the low oxygen, high-altitude environment has taken a toll on his health. He is received by a jeep with his probation ustad sitting in it. Daniel is told to change into his combats and a twenty-kilogram backpack is handed over to him. He is curtly told to put it on his back and start running towards the unit location which is twenty-one kilometres away. It takes Daniel three hours to walk-run to the unit with the jeep following him. 'From the moment your training starts, you are aware that you are being watched for any sign of weakness—physical or mental,' he says.

It is nearing 5 a.m. when a completely exhausted and breathless Daniel arrives at the unit campus. He is sent to the barracks where he has to live with the jawans for the next three months. After a one-hour break and a hefty breakfast of puri sabzi and chai, Daniel reports to Major Amitabh Valvalkar, his probation officer, trying to ignore the pain in his knees, ankles and shoulder. The Major points to the training programme pinned to a board on the wall and tells Daniel to follow the schedule.

There are three more officers and twenty soldiers doing the probation along with Daniel. They don't know then that they will not be allowed to sleep for the next two weeks. Through the day, the men are kept busy with intense physical training and through the night with assignments. They have to write essays on topics like the history of India's Special Forces, operations conducted by PARA, operations conducted by Special Forces in other countries, militant groups operating in Nagaland or Jammu and Kashmirand so on. They have the unit library with internet connectivity at their disposal. 'We seldom got to sleep for more than two to four hours each day. They were testing us for sincerity, endurance and mental toughness,' says Daniel.

Volunteers are taught six skills that include demolition, communication, medical, navigation, weapons training and tactics. They are trained in each skill for one-and-a-half weeks and the volunteers are tested after each unit. They also have to clear a physical test every day. On the tenth day they are asked to run ten kilometres, on the twentieth day twenty kilometres, and on the thirtieth day, they are asked to run thirty kilometres. On the fortieth day, it is forty kilometres carrying a thirty-kilogram backpack. Besides this, the probationers have to do navigation exercises, swimming tests and eighty-kilometre navigation walks.

'The first two weeks are pure torture,' says Daniel, 'Then slowly, your body and mind start getting used to it. You start believing you can take anything now. The non-PARA volunteer form is in your pocket at all times and right from the officers to the NCOs (non-commissioned officers) to the housekeeper to the chef, everyone keeps taunting you that you should fill it and leave. If you are ever caught slacking, you are penalized.' Once, when a completely sleep-deprived Daniel was caught dozing off in class, he was sent to a swamp and made to do front and side rolls in the dirty, stinking muck.

Daniel admits that he frequently had second thoughts about quitting and going home. But the constant provocation to leave just made him more determined to prove himself. Not everyone is as tough. Out of the three other officers with him, one gives up in the second week, another is asked to leave after three months and eventually, only two make it to the Special Forces. Out of the thirty soldiers who do the probation course, only twelve are selected. 'The selection process is so stringent that out of twenty-five officers who came for the course in 2012–13—the two years when I was there in the unit—only one was selected, says Daniel, who has also been an instructor for that probation course. 'We don't compromise on standards at all.'

More than expertise in a particular discipline, the men are tested for mental toughness. 'Out of two volunteers, an excellent swimmer who cannot stand in cold water through the night will be rejected, while a not-so-great swimmer who has the endurance to stand in that freezing water through the night will be selected. We are looking for men who will not give up in tough times—people with a cheerful disposition, with the ability to take pressure, with willpower and tenacity.'

He gives an example of how endurance is tested. 'We did a thirty-kilometre speed march carrying thirty-kilogram backpacks. The passing time given to us was three hours and thirty minutes. We were counting the minutes for it to end so that we could get a hot shower and maybe a nap but the moment we reached the finish line, we were told to go on another ten- kilometre navigation march. Our instructors were also gauging how we reacted to extra pressure because there might come a day when you would be required to do this in an enemy area. You just have to push yourself all the time,' he explains.

The volunteers are also given urban sector training. They have to rappel down from buildings, break into closed rooms and be prepared to fight terrorists holed up in an urban environment. At the end of the probation, the men are judged for their integrity, sincerity, initiative, decision-making skills, courage and willpower. Assessment forms are also filled up by colleagues as well as instructors and if a single person says no, the volunteer is rejected.

The training doesn't end there. At the end of the course, volunteers are sent for an actual operation and are tested in a real-life scenario. This is their last assessment sheet. Daniel's probation ended with him being sent on a seventy-two-hour operation with PARA (SF) in Manipur. 'We lived off the land for seventy-two hours, combing the jungles for three days, chasing militants who had killed two Assam Rifles jawans. We finally managed to apprehend them. I got the chance to participate in a firefight where we killed two militants and injured three,' he says. When the men returned to the unit location, Daniel found all the officers gathered there with a maroon beret and gigantic mug of punch. The beret was dipped in the alcohol and then placed on his head, much to his pride. He was then asked to drink up the lethal concoction even as everyone applauded him. 'That was the best moment of my life,' he says, his eyes shining with pleasure.

Daniel says the past six years with the Special Forces have been very satisfying. 'I got to represent the country in a joint Special Forces competition in Germany, I went to Bhutan on a mission and I got to train with Garud and Marcos (the Air Force and Navy commandos). I have also trained with the US Special Forces. This is the kind of life I always wanted,' he says. He is now with PARA (SF) a new raising of the Indian Army, posted in an undisclosed location in Kashmir. When I ask him to check his email for the quotes I have sent him he says he won't be able to do it since he doesn't know when he will be in an area with internet coverage. Wishing him the best of luck, I hang up the phone. Major John Daniel is on the call of duty.

The toughest guys in the Army

Special Forces are the GI Joes of the Indian Army. They are the men who can skydive, deep-sea dive, operate all kinds of weapons and are well-versed in close combat. They know no fears, and are ready to put their lives on line for a cause, which is why the badge they earn is called 'Balidaan' or sacrifice. Those who serve in the Special Forces say they all have one thing in common—there are some wires loose in all their heads. It is a tough life, full of excitement and opportunities to be James Bond but only the toughest can make it. If you think you have it in you, then here's what you need to do.

Special Forces are a voluntary force. A few vacancies come out each year for which a GC can opt directly from the Academy, or even later, after being allotted a unit. So far, women are not admitted into the Special Forces. Volunteers are put through a probationary period selection process of six months for PARA (Special Forces) battalions. All volunteers are first required to qualify as paratroopers. Once selected as a paratrooper, the candidate may choose to advance to the selection, which takes place about four times in the year, depending on how many candidates apply.

It is one of the longest and toughest probations in the world where the applicant is exposed to sleep deprivation, humiliation, exhaustion, mental and physical extremes. The attrition rate is very high and selection rarely exceeds 10 per cent. Even though a candidate may have cleared selection, he is not inducted into the regiment formally until the completion of the 'Balidaan Padh' in which a trained candidate is sent for an active operation in a hostile zone. If he proves himself, he is given the Balidaan badge and formally inducted into the regiment, by placing a maroon beret dipped in rum punch on his head.

A tough training

All men are trained in using arms including pistols, machine guns, assault rifles, carbines, Kalashnikovs, grenade launchers and rocket launchers. They are expert swimmers and free-fallers. The commandos are trained for combat on land, air and water. Taught skills include infiltration and exfiltration by air and sea, the free fall course, which requires at least fifty jumps from altitudes up to 33,500 feet, where they have to sometimes jump with oxygen cylinders and in the night. Both HALO (High Altitude Low Opening) and HAHO (High Altitude High Opening) techniques are taught to them. For combat diving training, the commandos are sent to the Naval Diving School, Kochi.

Training includes long-distance runs stretching to twenty kilometres, intelligence-gathering, patrolling, ambush tactics, counter-insurgency, counter-terrorism, unconventional warfare, guerilla warfare, raids and sabotage, martial arts, close-quarter battle, advance weapon courses, sniping, demolition training, survival skills, linguistics, among others. The training drills involve live ammunition at all times. The Special Forces conduct annual exercises with other countries, including the US, Israel, UK, France, Russia, Mongolia, Kazakhstan, Uzbekistan, Kyrgyzstan, Bangladesh, Myanmar, Nepal, Maldives, Seychelles, Singapore, Indonesia and Thailand.

Popular Myths Busted

Do you think the Army is not for the bright bunch? That women can't be rifle shooters? That it ends your dreams of travelling abroad? You couldn't be more wrong! Let's have a look at some of these myths!

17

'It's not a career for women!'

Myth: It's not a career for women.
Reality: Major Raj Chaudhary, Engineer Regiment, Corps of
Engineers, daughter, mom, wife and national-level shooter.

'There are some promises that we make to ourselves too . . .'

November 2016
Naseerabad

Dawn is breaking over the Army cantonment near Ajmer when the silence of the morning is interrupted by the soft tread of sneakers hitting the road. A lone runner in trackpants and a thin sweater, a neat plait falling over her shoulders, is painstakingly jogging her way through the chilly winter morning. Her warm breath comes out like a jet of steam in the cold, the sound of her heavy, strained breathing puncturing the quiet.

A little plump and out of practice, national-level shooter Major Raj Chaudhary of Engineer Regiment is getting back in shape for the competition coming up in two months. Since she has recently had a baby, Raj has a lot of fitness training to catch up on. She will be going back to shooting after a long break. 'It's like starting from scratch once again,' she says candidly. 'I can barely run one kilometre at a stretch now. But I have decided I will get back in form.'

Besides being a new mother, Chaudhary is also an Army wife and an only daughter to ageing parents who live with her. But above all, she is an Army officer with a steely will. 'Yes, I have a lot of responsibilities towards a lot of people,' she says, looking into my eyes. 'Par kuch vaade hum apne aap se bhi karte hain. (There are some promises that we make to ourselves.)'

A gun decided what I wanted to do in life

Raj's love affair with guns starts when she is nineteen years old. An outstanding student, she is studying for a physics honours degree from Kirori Mal College in New Delhi with ambitions of becoming an IAS officer. Around the same time, a classmate coaxes her into joining the NCC at Miranda House since her own college does not have NCC for girls.

There, at a Combat Engineering Training Camp (CETC) in 2003, she touches a gun for the very first time. 'It was like love at first touch,' she smiles. 'Frankly speaking, I had never been into sports. I didn't play any games or do any physical activity. I was a complete bookworm but the moment I held a gun, I knew this was what I wanted to do in life.' She did surprisingly well for someone who had never handled a rifle before and was amongst the four girls selected for the national championships.

'That was the first time I found out about the Olympics, the Commonwealth Games and National Games selections,' she says. Unfortunately, she cannot go for the National Games selections because it means missing college for a month and the head of the physics department tells her she will not be given marks for the practicals for the time she is away. 'I couldn't go but it helped me decide that shooting was what I wanted to do in life.'

When she discusses her newfound passion with her father, Naik Saudan Singh Chaudhary, a boxer and weightlifter in the Army who has taken voluntary retirement, he advises her that the Army is the only place where she can indulge this passion for shooting. That strikes a chord with Raj. 'I thought if I join the Army, I will get to shoot,' she says. The fire has been lit! She starts physical training in preparation for the Army Services Selection Board (SSB) and even though she passes the IAS preliminary, she does not write the main examinations because she now wants to be an Army officer.

Training for the Army

2006, Nangloi

Every Sunday morning, Raj Chaudhary, sleeping peacefully in her bed, is shaken awake by her father and sent running.

Her training to join the Army has begun. The well-built and grey-haired Naik Saudan Singh cycles down to the mango orchard, around two kilometres from their house, keeping pace with his daughter who is huffing and puffing alongside. Each time she stops, he also stops and hollers 'Shabash! Aage badho!' at her, and she starts running again. 'In the beginning, I couldn't even run one kilometre,' Raj confesses. 'I would just hold my cramped, aching stomach and wait for him to yell at me. But slowly my stamina started increasing.'

The distance to the orchard is not counted as exercise. Once there, her father makes her do two kilometres of running around the orchard. After that, she does sit-ups on the ground and soon after that, her father makes her use the monkey bars in the park to do sit-ups while hanging from her knees. At the end of the session, Raj desperately waits for her mother to bring breakfast for the whole family. They sit down together under the trees and eat, throwing crumbs to the chirping birds and squirrels.

After completing her graduation, Raj clears her SSB written exams, a cakewalk for her since she is a very good student. The physical exams in Bhopal are much tougher than expected but the strict training her father put her through helps her sail through those as well. 'My father didn't even come with me to Bhopal,' she says. 'He sent me there alone and told me to be independent.' He was just reiterating a lesson he had taught her early in life. He hadn't gone with her for her college admissions either. And even earlier, when she was in Class VIII and had come crying to him after a love-struck classmate had given her a romantic letter, he had refused to intervene, curtly telling her to handle it on her own. 'If you want to reply to the letter, go ahead and write a reply. If you want to slap him, go back and slap him,' he had said, making the feisty Raj so angry that she had gone back to school, found the boy and given him a tight slap. 'I was relieved when he didn't hit me back,' she says. 'Perhaps it was because I was the class monitor!'

A few years later in Delhi, she slaps a roadside Romeo who has the audacity to grasp her hand when she is returning home late one evening from college—only to be slapped back by him. They have a physical fight but Raj manages to snatch his bike keys and take him to the nearest police station, helped by the gathered crowd. From there she calls her father, who comes to the police station almost immediately, proud of his bold daughter. 'We registered an FIR but took it back when the boy apologized profusely and promised never to trouble a girl again,' she says.

Officer at twenty-one

There aren't too many girls who don't want to put on weight because then they won't fit into their shooting rig, or who spend all their money on guns, and then laugh that they don't have any left for anything else. Raj Chaudhary does. She has always been a soldier first. When Raj got through the SSB and was going to join the OTA in Chennai, her father didn't tell her to take care, to eat well or to not get hurt training. He gruffly warned her not to let him down by running away from the Academy. And she didn't. When she returned home, she was a smartly dressed young Lieutenant with a blue Engineers beret on her head and two stars on each shoulder, which made her father's eyes moist with pride. At the Academy, her talent for shooting was recognized and she was contacted by the Army Marksmanship Unit (AMU). They promised to call her soon. Meanwhile, she joined Engineer Regiment in Tezpur, Assam. In 2008 she was sent for her Young Officers course to Army War College (AWC), Mhow, with the gentle admonition from senior officers in her unit: 'Don't come back with a Charlie (C) grading.'

She scored an AI (Instructor, the highest grading in the Army). 'I had no problem learning about mines, bridging, demolition and other aspects from reading slides. My physics honours degree had been a much tougher course,' she laughs. Soon after she got back to Tezpur, her AMU attachment also came through and in August 2009 she left for Mhow once again; this time to formally be trained as a shooter.

On her first day at the shooting range, her coach mistook her for a professional shooter and asked her to hold her gun in the holding position for half an hour. It is an exercise that shooters do to establish control over their mind and weapon. She did it but her arm became numb soon after and she couldn't even straighten her fingers. That was when her coach realized that though she was very good shooter, she was still an amateur. He was really impressed with her determination since it was a very difficult exercise for even seasoned shooters to do.

At the end of the month, from the fifteen lady officers selected by the AMU, eight were sent back to their units but

Raj was not one of them. She says she had decided from day one that she had not come to the AMU to go back. Raj was amongst the three lady officers who finally qualified for the National Games. She won a gold medal for the fifty-metre prone event at the 2009 pre-national games in Asansol but she couldn't qualify for the event she had been training for—the ten-metre air rifle. She was heartbroken but did not give up. In 2013, she won the gold again in the pre-nationals and came fourth in the National Games. In the 2014 National Games, she established a new record for the ten-metre air rifle. She shot 208.8 score at the final, the highest ever shot by any athlete till then, and was given the Best Athlete Award.

Training to shoot

'Shooters need a lot of control over their thoughts,' explains Raj. 'One small emotion or thought can affect the event completely. We have to learn to control our minds.' Following a strict regimen of yoga, meditation and physical training helps she says. When shooters are firing, there is a lot of shouting going on in the background. They have to learn to control their thoughts so that the shouting does not distract them. 'We have to be removed from anything happening around us, and we need a lot of practice to keep calm in all situations.'

The first time she was pitched against shooters with fourteen years of shooting experience, she was unnerved but then she realized that the more pressure you put on yourself, the more you learn. Raj says she has come a long way from the girl who had never held a rifle in her hands. She started with innate talent and hard work but the Army gave her the exposure, the coaches, the encouragement and the opportunities that turned a bookworm into a famous shooter. She has no plans to stop though there have been major events in between. She met and married Major Pankaj Kumar Mishra, a handsome Sapper officer from her own regiment, and has adopted Tiger and Gorgeous, two golden-brown Labrador puppies who are now just a little jealous of the new baby in her life, her two-month-old daughter, Anaysha.

Amongst her other prized possessions are a slick and shining Bleiker rifle for fifty-metre shooting events that cost her Rs 5.6 lakhs, a Walther Anatomic air rifle for ten-metre events worth Rs 2.5 lakhs and a shooting kit that includes jackets, trousers and shoes worth Rs 1.5 lakhs. 'If I put on weight, I can't get into my kit, and that's another incentive for losing weight,' Raj says. Other than these precious possessions, she has nothing in the bank, she claims. From her ringing laughter it is obvious that she doesn't mind that at all. On a more serious note, she says that the most difficult thing for a sportsperson to do is to stay motivated. 'We need to be motivated all the time because at every step your mind says "Stop" but your heart coaxes you to take one more step. You can take the next step only if you are motivated.'

Her advice to all those who want to pursue adventure sports or rifle shooting or join the NCC or the Army or pick up a career off the beaten path is, 'If you want to do something different, just go for it! Be passionate about whatever you want and more often than not, it shall come to you.' She has a message for girls too. 'Don't let any person or any inhibitions stop you from reaching for the dream you have seen for yourself. Make some promises to yourself and fulfil them,' she says. Raj herself is aiming for the 2020 Olympics.

Mission Olympics

'If you are passionate about sports and the Olympics is your dream, come to us—we will train you for it,' says Colonel Amit Bisht, Director, Mission Olympics, making a very tempting offer to potential Army officers. Sitting in his office at Sena Bhawan in New Delhi, the soft-spoken and smiling Colonel Bisht, who is himself an avid mountaineer and helicopter pilot with 3,500 flying hours to his credit, tells me about the programme he heads that offers unbelievable opportunities to sportspersons within the Army.

The Directorate General of Military Training started Mission Olympics in the year 2001. It was initiated with the aim of picking and training the best sportspersons in the Army and helping them reach the Olympics. One of the most famous trainees of the programme is Colonel Rajyavardhan Singh Rathore, AVSM, who created history at the Athens Olympics in 2004 by becoming the first-ever Indian to win a silver medal in an individual sporting event for shooting. This feat was repeated by Subedar Major Vijay Kumar, AVSM, SM, who won another silver medal for shooting at the London Olympics in 2012.

'We coordinate with the Sports Authority of India,' says Bisht, talking about how they identify and groom sportspersons. 'We identify young soldiers and officers who are promising at a particular sport. They are then given the chance to work with the best coaches and train in the country and abroad.' This is done through five Mission Olympics nodes across India, including the Army Sports Institute at Pune, where around 551 top Army sportsmen are being trained in the disciplines of athletics, archery, boxing, diving, fencing, weightlifting and wrestling. Other nodes are the AMU in Mhow, where around 128 ace shooters of the Army are under training; the Army Rowing Node in Pune, where eighty-five Army rowers are being trained; the Army Yachting Node in Mumbai, where fifty-six Army sailors are under training and the Army Equestrian Node in Meerut, that has world-class training infrastructure for showjumping, dressage and cross-country and is currently conducting training camps for thirty-nine horse riders. 'Sports climbing is a new discipline that we have identified,' says Bisht. This is a sport that will be played at the Tokyo Olympics in 2020 for the first time and the Army team is training for it in the Wellington cantonment where artificial walls have been created.

Many of the sportspersons training at the Mission Olympics nodes have won national awards. In 2016, Subedar Jitu Rai, SM, won the Rajiv Gandhi Khel Ratna Award; Subedar Gurpreet Singh won the Arjuna Award, both for shooting; and Subedar R.P. Shelka won the Dhyanchand Award for rowing. Major Raj Chaudhary is a promising shooter with a very impressive medal tally so far in the National Games. Captain Ruchi Trikha has put in a wonderful performance in fencing and is being trained for the Olympics.

How do young officers join Mission Olympics?

'We pick officers who are already performing the sport, or those who may have a flair for it. The Army promotes sports in a big way and routine inter-unit, inter-brigade and inter-command competitions help us identify good sportspersons. These are then given a chance at the national-level competitions. From this pool of good sportspersons, the best are trained further. We are taking our training to Olympic levels,' explains Bisht.

'Trainers at our nodes are Olympians, sports professionals and coaches from India and abroad. We are investing in giving our sportspersons the best support we can. Right from infrastructure to dieticians and from doctors to specialists, our facilities are the best in every discipline and no expenses are spared,' he adds. 'In coordination with the Sports Authority of India, elite sportspersons are also taken for international competitions to give them the best exposure. We take care of everything for the athlete from buying their tickets to arranging their stay to sending officers for administrative support. The sportsperson just needs to concentrate on their sport. Which other institution will do all this for you?' he asks with a winning smile.

Mission Olympics has its sights set on the Tokyo Olympics. 'Our sportspersons are training hard for it,' he says. 'Wait and watch!'

18

'It's a no-brain job!'

Myth—You don't need to be smart to be in the Army.
Reality—Major Shailesh Tripathi, Corps of Signals, white hat,
computer expert and cyber warrior.

'The warriors of the future might never carry a gun . . .'

Envisioned war scene
Sometime in the future; the open seas.

Picture this—it is wartime. Friendly ships are heading towards their own country under the darkness of night after a long-drawn-out military operation. Thousands of miles away, a hacker fiddling with her laptop intercepts their radar identifiers and changes them. To the home country, it suddenly appears that enemy ships are headed in their direction. An alarm is raised, guns readied for attack and the approaching ships are fired upon, bringing them down in flames, causing mass destruction and death. There is jubilation in the naval units till search parties are sent out to the wreckage to assess damage. It leads to the shocking discovery that they have shot down their own men who were unsuspectingly coming home. No one knows how the confusion occurred.

'That may be the future of war,' says Mahendra Singh Negi, chief financial officer, Trend Micro, an IT security company that handles internet content security for the armed forces of various countries. Disclosing that Trend Micro researchers have successfully managed to change the radar identifiers of ships and aircraft, Negi is quick to mention, 'Our ground rule is we only defend and never attack or help in attacking.' Though emphasizing that his company never hires an unethical hacker and would never provide such technology to others, Negi has given us a frightening glimpse of how wars in the future could be fought. 'The warriors of the future might never carry a gun,' he says.

It's no wonder then that armies across the world are looking at recruiting brilliant young men and women who can also be cyber warriors. These are soldiers who might never have to go out with guns and grenades—they will use their laptops to defend their country by pre-empting and intercepting cyberattacks. If you have the aptitude to be such a soldier, the Army needs you.

Major Shailesh Tiwary from the Corps of Signals is a cyber warrior. 'Cyberspace is the fifth dimension after land, air, water and space. This is where the wars of the future will be fought,' he tells me, emphasizing that cyber threats are now viewed as the number one threat to world security. 'The US compiles a list of top ten threats to world security every year,' he says. 'Until the year 2007, there was no mention of cyber threats—terrorism was at number one. In 2012, cyber threats showed up at number thirteen for the first time and from 2013 onwards, they have been featuring as threat number one, towering above terrorism, drug trafficking and weapons of mass destruction.'

It is possible that enemies sitting halfway across the globe will be able to sabotage our servers, satellites, airplanes, trains and communication modes and we won't even know who they are. Future cyberattacks could be launched against nuclear power plants, military bases, business houses or electrical power grids. All a hacker needs is a computer and an internet connection to makes planes crash, cities go dark and cold, railways to stop functioning and even explosions to take place in our own nuclear plants.

Cyberattacks will be used to jam radars, disable infrared detection, plant viruses on foreign computers to destroy sensitive data. That is why the Army needs experts in the field. Cyber warfare is already here and attacks will continue to increase in frequency and intensity. Lone hackers who live on the fringe of anonymity will be sought and recruited by armies. The need for soldiers on ground will decline and it will even the playing field. Even small countries with access to computers and some sharp brain power will be able to attack a larger country with a massive military presence. Moonlight Maze, Slammer, Titan Rain and Ghostnet attacks over the past decade have shown that cyberattacks are a real and present danger across the world.

Slammer is a worm that hit at 5.30 am on 25 January 2003. It is known as the fastest cyberattack in history. According to a team of researchers, the number of infections doubled every 8.5 seconds and Slammer did the maximum damage in the first ten minutes of its release. Among other things, the worm took down parts of the internet in South Korea and Japan, disrupted phone services in Finland, and slowed down airline reservations systems, credit card networks and automatic teller machines in the US. According to the presidential advisor for cyberspace security, Slammer could have done much more damage. The fact that it didn't led to the suspicion that it was just a test to see what damage could have been done. Something that could be used in the next attack.

The scariest thing about cyberattacks is their non-accountability. You don't know who attacked you or from where. 'Often, you don't even find out that you have been a target,' says Tiwary. 'Sitting here today, I can attack a country and make it appear as if some other country has done it.'

In March 2015, the Indian Army's Comptroller of Defence Accounts (CDA) website was hacked. Officers could not access their accounts and there were fears that sensitive data had been stolen. Tiwary was then on the computer emergency response team (CERT). 'We hacked the hacker, exposed the breach and capped it,' he says. 'If we had not been on the job, we would never have found out that the security breach had taken place and all our sensitive defence data could have been stolen.'

Tiwary says he was always an internet nerd. 'It was my area of interest since I was very young,' he admits. He joined the Army after Class XII through the Army's Technical Entry Scheme (TES). After a four-year engineering degree at the Cadet Training Wing at the Military College of Telecommunication Engineering (MCTE) in Mhow, where he attended the TES Course, he also spent one year at the IMA in Dehradun. He graduated as a young Lieutenant and at his first posting at Ambala with the Grid Signal Regiment he was responsible for the IT set-up of the entire cantonment.

'My job was to set up this network and ensure that it worked properly,' he says. From there he went on to dismantling advanced persistent threats (APTs) and deciphering modus operandi of information security operations driven by malicious intent. 'I have studied information security for more than fourteen years now,' says Tiwary. 'My time with the Indian Army has given me wide exposure to defending critical information assets and engineering security overlays. I have mobilized information security operations to thwart malicious hacking campaigns launched by our enemies in cyberspace. My role demands the continuous learning of new techniques and technologies as I keep pace with the current digital threat-scape.'

Tiwary says cyber threats have really risen in the recent past and armies across the world are seriously looking at recruiting hackers as cyber warriors. To do so seriously, the respective army will need to relax their rules, he says. 'People who have a special talent for hacking might not necessarily be good at studies or communication,' he says. 'Cyber warriors are sometimes nerdy and unsocial, and prefer to work behind the cloak of anonymity. No school teaches you hacking so these hackers are likely to be the self-taught IT geniuses who are not necessarily good at other subjects. Hence, one might have to eventually make waivers for hiring cyber talent,' he admits.

So if you are good with computers and would like to be an ethical hacker, you could consider joining the Corps of Signals. 'Your hobby will become your profession, and you will get a chance to defend your country in cyberspace,' says Tiwary. To join the Corps of Signals, you'll need to write the CDS exam and join the NDA or the IMA, opting for a career in IT and communication within the Army. Major Tiwary is back in the MCTE as faculty, and he now trains Army officers to defend India in cyberspace. 'I'm responsible for training both technical and executive staff in fifth-dimension operations to prepare them for digital D-Day,' he says. Tiwary is also a recipient of the COAS's commendation card for exemplary performance in the domain of cyber security during his tenure in the Indian Army's CERT.

Flying a drone

While cyber warfare is a war waged through digital weapons, remote-controlled warfare might also sound interesting to you, particularly if you are a video game buff. As a soldier, you would operate by sending digital commands to physical agents, namely drones, which would then attack the enemy soldiers. This is a battle in which humans would only be holding the controls. India is using drones and sooner or later this will progress to step two by morphing into battles where our physical agents would be attacking the enemy's physical agents (for example our remote-controlled tanks would be attacking the enemy's remote-controlled tanks) and no humans would be involved in the battle at all. It would be a war scenario that would be like playing a video game.

The Indian Army has drones, both armed and surveillance versions, which are operated by specially trained officers. The state-run Defence Research and Development Organization (DRDO) has also developed indigenous unmanned drones like Rustom and Nishant under its Unmanned Air Vehicle (UAV) programme. Rustom-II, which weighs 1,800 kilograms, can carry a payload of 350 kilograms and remain airborne for thirty-six hours at a stretch. Nishant is also a multi-mission UAV with day/night capability. It is used for battlefield surveillance and reconnaissance (ISR), target tracking and localization and artillery fire correction.

Drones provide world-class intelligence, ISR capabilities to a country. Armed drones are intended to expand the response options available to the Indian military as it has to mount more operations to neutralize terrorist elements based out of remote facilities in neighbouring countries. The employment of armed drones for precision strikes will also make it easier for the Indian military to neutralize targets in scenarios where sending in the Special Forces would be too risky or complicated. To be a drone flier in the Army, you have to opt for Artillery in the IMA. After you get a unit and join, you can apply for a UAV course.

The Corps of Signals

The Corps of Signals is an arm of the Indian Army which handles military communications. It was formed on 15 February 1911, initially for the purpose of passing messages in the battlefield. Until then, the Sappers from the Indian Army Corps of Engineers used to be responsible for this. The first signal units to be raised at Fatehgarh, Uttar Pradesh, were the 31st and 32nd Divisional Signal Companies. The founder of the Indian Signal Service, which later came to be known as the Indian Signal Corps, was Lieutenant Colonel S.H. Powell of the Royal Engineers. After the wars of 1965 and 1971, the Corps of Signals underwent a massive expansion. Responsibilites have widened largely since then and include cyber warfare, which is a rising concern for armies across the world.

The Corps of Signals works closely with the DRDO to develop software for command and control. One of its major contibutions is the Samyukta Electronic Warfare System, a mobile integrated electronic warfare system that was developed in collaboration with Bharat Electronics Limited. Signal officers are trained at the MCTE, Mhow.

19

'It grounds your dreams of going abroad.'

Myth—Joining the Army means a lifetime spent on the borders of the country.
Reality—Colonel Sunil Sheoran, SM, from PARA (Special Forces) has been sent to nineteen countries during his twenty-five years in uniform.

Ask Colonel Sunil Sheoran, SM, about his most interesting memory of the armed forces of the nineteen other countries that the Indian Army has sent him to and he breaks into a chuckle. 'A cricket match,' he says.

During a Higher Command course to Australia in 2013, Sheoran was one of nineteen students from different armies around the world. The course strength was forty-two, the rest being made up of Australian Army officers. 'One day the Australians came up with the idea that we should have a friendly cricket match followed by lunch, with the locals pitched against the foreign students. The Australians were, of course, sure they would win. Our team had students from Indonesia, China, Canada, Germany, Egypt and Thailand,' Sheoran recounts. 'All these guys had never played cricket and so naturally, we were a bit jittery about the match,' he says.

The Australians put up a grand score and when it was the foreign students' team's turn, there were loud cheers from the home team, confident about handing out a crushing defeat. They put up a stiff fight but were losing as expected, with one batsman getting out after the other in quick succession. The Pakistani officer and Sheoran were the last to bat. 'We put up a stiff fight since we were the only two who had played cricket. We didn't do badly but on the last ball we needed a six to win,' remembers Sheoran. 'I was on the runner's side and I walked up to the Pakistani officer and told him, "My friend, this time we fight on the same side and we have to win." The Pakistani officer grinned back and voila! He hit a six much to the delight of the rest of the team. 'The Aussies were so shocked by this freak win that they couldn't even have lunch,' Sheoran remembers, smiling widely.

Colonel Sheoran, from PARA (Special Forces) has been to nineteen countries on various Army courses and appointments in his twenty-five years in uniform. 'You can join the Army and see the world,' he says. 'But believe me— saare jahan se accha, Hindustan hamara.'

Nicknamed 'Bullet Catcher' by his colleagues for his tendency to attract action (he was shot twice in a span of two years right in the beginning of his career), Colonel Sunil Sheoran has many claims to fame but today, he's dispelling the myth for us that Army officers only get to see the borders of the country. Before that, however, we need to hear an action story and he obliges with one that happened early in his career.

Sheoran and three of his Naga soldiers were on a dangerous mission chasing Naga insurgents in a village near the Nagaland–Assam border. 'We were all dressed in jeans and Naga shawls to stay undercover. While the Naga boys could pass for locals, I thought I could be mistaken for a trader,' he remembers. 'Imagine our surprise when we went closer to the insurgents, who were much larger in number, and realized that they were all dressed in olive-green. It was an amusing role reversal, where the enemy was in uniform and the Army was in civvies.' After a long and heated chase, the outnumbered soldiers finally got some back-up support from another team of soldiers from their unit. 'When the supporting team asked me for directions, I told them, "We are all in civvies; just shoot anyone you find dressed in Army combats." And that's what they did,' Sheoran says, laughing heartily.

Over the years, he's been shot a number of times and the bullets that have left a mark on him—one above the heart, another in the shoulder, and yet another one that went through his cheek and neck. Sheoran has also served at Darshak, the highest post in the Siachen Glacier (19,000 feet) and led the National Security Guard (NSG) team during the hostage rescue in the Taj Mahal Hotel in Mumbai on 26 November 2008. However, with his stints to nineteen different countries, he is a poster boy for world travel. Congo,

Australia, the US, South Korea, Indonesia, France, Germany, China, Papua New Guinea—you run out of fingers ticking off his travels abroad.

He tells me an amusing story about the time he took a team of Indian Army combat free fallers to the US for a joint exercise. Most Indian soldiers come from villages and know very little English and naturally, they found conversation difficult with the Americans who did not know any Hindi. 'My team consisted of Haryanvis, Garhwalis and Gorkhas amongst other Indian communities,' he says. During a night jump exercise, the American Sergeant on the jump was worried if the Indian soldiers had understood his instructions or not—he feared they might get lost in the darkness.

After the jump, Sheoran went to check if all his men had reached safely and was happy to find them all there. When he conveyed this to the men, they started laughing sheepishly. They told him they were so afraid of getting lost because they did not know enough English to ask for directions that they decided that they would stay together even in the air. That's how the entire team landed together at the dropping zone with perfect precision, something they had never done in India. 'Saab gum jaate toh kya hota, (What if we lost our way?)' they told him when he went around slapping their backs. 'The funny thing was that some of the American paratroopers got lost that night,' Sheoran chuckles.

It's been a great run in the Army and Sheoran has one piece of advice for all youngsters today: 'Join the Army, work hard, do well in your courses and the chances are that you will get to see the world. Also with time, the opportunities that you get in the Army are only increasing,' he says. A very good student right from school, Sheoran had cleared the MBBS entrance exam but decided to join the NDA to follow in the footsteps of his father Lieutenant Colonel Sher Singh, VC.

In the NDA, he stood fourth in a course of 280 cadets and at the IMA, he stood seventh in a course of 400 Gentlemen Cadets. Highly impressed with his adjutant at the IMA, who was from the Special Forces, Sheoran opted for PARA (SF) and made it through the extremely tough selection and probation process. A few years later, when he returned to the NDA as an instructor, history repeated itself. 'Half of the cadets wanted to join the Special Forces influenced by me,' he laughs.

Sheoran's first international experience came when he was sent to Congo on a UN Mission. 'I was appointed military observer and it was a great learning experience and exposure to the working of the UN.' Three years later, Sheoran got the opportunity to take a Special Forces team of free fallers to the US for joint exercises with the American Special Forces. In 2013, he was selected for the Army's Higher Command course, and being one of the best performers in his course, he was also sent to the Centre for Defence and Strategic Studies (CDSS), Australia, where he opted to do his masters in strategic studies from Deakin University.

'Higher Command is a promotional course that officers undergo in the Army before being promoted to the rank of Brigadier. Four officers are picked from each course for a foreign university education—I was one of them.' Along with the other Higher Command officers, he also went on a study tour to visit countries like China, South Korea, Indonesia, and Papua New Guinea. This is routine exposure that all Higher Command officers are given. 'The four-country tour is aimed at providing a better understanding of how armies in the rest of the world function,' he explains.

After the NSG successfully neutralized the terrorist threat at the Taj Mahal Hotel, the Trident Oberoi and Nariman House in Mumbai on 26 November 2008, a decision was taken by the government to establish NSG hubs across the country and Sheoran travelled to France, Israel, Germany and the US as part of that process. He interacted with the world's best hostage rescue and counter-terrorism units like GSG-9 (Germany), GIGN/RAID (France), Special SWAT Units (Australia) and YAMAM (Israel).

Married to Major Dr Sween Sheoran, a doctor who opted to join the Army so that she could spend more time with her husband, Colonel Sheoran is presently looking after his two kids, aged eight and twelve, on his own in Delhi. 'There has been a role reversal,' he says. 'These days, Sween is on a UN mission to Sudan and I've been posted to Army Headquarters, Delhi, and am looking after the kids.'

Besides being a hands-on father, Sheoran is also an avid microlight pilot and free faller. 'Being in the Army has given me the chance to explore whatever opportunities I have wanted to increase my knowledge both in service of the nation and for personal fulfilment. The Army has literally taken me around the world,' he says. 'In the future, UN Missions will increase; there will be more courses, more defence engagements and joint exercises with other countries. Young people opting for the Army will get more and more opportunities to travel abroad.'

Operation Black Tornado

No reference to Colonel Sunil Sheoran would be complete without mentioning the fact that he was commanding the elite counter-terrorism unit, 51 Special Action Group, NSG when the Mumbai terror attacks shook the nation in November 2008. Ten members of Lashkar-e-Taiba, an Islamic militant organization based in Pakistan, perpetuated acts of terror and death in Mumbai over three days of shooting and bomb attacks. The senseless violence began on 26 November and lasted till 29 November, killing 164 people and wounding 308. The NSG was called in to neutralize the terrorists who had taken hostages inside hotels and were putting them to death.

An expert in counter-terrorism and special operations, Sheoran led his group during this mission called Operation Black Tornado. The fearless commandos blazed their way inside the Taj Mahal Hotel, the Oberoi and Nariman House and successfully neutralized nine terrorists. The final operation at the Taj Mahal Hotel was completed by the NSG commandos at 8 a.m. on 29 November, killing the last three terrorists. They rescued 250 people from the Oberoi, 300 from the Taj and 60 from Nariman House. They lost two bravehearts in the process—Major Sandeep Unnikrishnan and Havildar Gajendra Singh.

20

'I joined the Army at forty.'

Myth—If you're older than twenty, you can't join the Army.
Reality—Lieutenant Manivanan P. of 106 Infantry Battalion
(TA) PARA, IAS and Army officer who picked up a Lieutenant's
rank at forty.

What do Lieutenant Colonel Mahendra Singh Dhoni and
Lieutenant Manivanan P. have in common? They are both
officers of the Indian Territorial Army (TA) in the same unit, 106
Infantry Battalion (TA) PARA. On most mornings, Lieutenant
Manivanan P., Secretary, Social Welfare Department,
Government of Karnataka, is a busy civil servant who works in
the Vidhan Sauda, Bengaluru. From 9 a.m. to 7 p.m., he chairs
meetings, takes decisions on serious matters and receives endless
visitors. Very few of those visiting his office know that this IAS
officer is also an Army officer who is trained to use an AK-56
rifle and that for two months in the year, he takes a break from
the civil services to command men in uniform.

During the two compulsory months every year that he serves as an Army officer, Mani dons his olive-green uniform, wears a belt and beret and adds Lieutenant in front of his name. He shifts to his unit's location in Benson Town, around 30 kilometres away from his Koramangala residence. Any important government files that need his signatures are then sent to him at the unit location where he lives in the bachelors' accommodation attached to the Officers Mess and works with the soldiers. 'Through the year too, I attend dining ins and outs of officers, social functions that I am invited for and am there for my unit whenever my CO Colonel Vrijendra Singh Lingwal needs me,' he says.

Mani says that, for him, being in the Army was like a dream that came true, even if a little later in life. 'When I was forty to be precise,' he smiles. Mani always wanted to be an Army officer. 'It was my first choice of career but unfortunately, my father did not allow me to apply for the NDA entrance test. He wanted me to become a doctor or an engineer,' he says. He didn't opt for either of those though and ended up completing his graduation and then passing the civil services entrance exams. 'The Army remained an unlived dream. For so many years, despite being an IAS officer, I had no idea that there was something called the Indian Territorial Army, and that I could still join the Army.' In the year 2013, a friend who was an Indian Revenue Service (IRS) officer joined TA and told Mani about it.

When he found out that he could still join the Army, Mani enthusiastically wrote the entrance test, cleared his SSB and reported for training at 106 Infantry Battalion (TA) PARA in Bengaluru. For one month, he underwent strict physical training that included drills, parades, physicals, running and learning how to fire weapons. At long last, on the afternoon of 8 February 2014, he was pipped in the unit Mess—on one shoulder by Station Commander Major General S.K. Singh and on the other by Mani's wife Salma Fahim, who is also an IAS officer. He joined the Army as a forty-year-old Lieutenant. 'It was a very proud moment for me,' he says. A childhood dream had finally come true!

'Till I joined the Army, I could not run even three kilometres,' he confesses but adds proudly, 'Now I usually go for a five-kilometre run in the morning and sometimes I stretch it to ten kilometres. My training has made me fitter, more conscious of my health, more active and more in control of my body.' Mani says he is confident that if his country needs him, he can easily don his uniform and do whatever is required from him as an Army officer. 'Even if they don't send me to fight on the border, I can still use my experience as a civil servant to handle many different things.'

Besides instilling physical toughness, there are two important things that the Army experience has taught him, he says. The first is to accept things without complaining. 'If I find myself in an unwelcome situation now, I respond positively. I have never heard an Army officer complaining. They might be posted to the toughest terrain, with no leave to be with family on festivals and birthdays, and they might have to stay in hot deserts or freezing cold mountains, but they just take it on the chin.' The other thing he has learnt is man management. 'In the civil set-up we cannot match the

Army's management of their human resources, and mind you, these are men with weapons in their hands who know how to use them.'

It must not be easy for a civil servant to take two months off each year to be an Army officer. Mani agrees. 'At my position, I have a lot a responsibilities and unfortunately there are only twenty-four hours in a day. But luckily, my state government understands how passionate I am about being able to serve my country and they have let me take that break every year.' As yet, Mani hasn't been able to do his one-month para probation at Agra, where he will be taught to jump from a plane and become a full-fledged paratrooper. 'I have been promised leave and shall complete that as soon as I can,' he says. The dual role does leave him short of time but he says he is lucky that his wife Salma who is also posted at Bengaluru, understands his passion for the Army. 'We often drive down thirty kilometres to be at the battalion when there is a compulsory social engagement and she accompanies me happily.' They have three children—Amogh, thirteen, Aadil, four, and Armaan, two. 'The boys are too young to understand things but I hope at least one of them will be inspired by the Army and join it too,' says Mani.

Joining the Indian Territorial Army

If you are in the age group of eighteen to forty-two years, a graduate and gainfully employed, you can join the TA. All you need to do is apply in response to advertisements published in leading national newspapers or the *Employment*

News (the weekly job magazine published by the Ministry of Information and Broadcasting) in May–June each year. The information is also available on the Army website (www. indianarmy.nic.in).

Completed applications are to be sent to the concerned TA Group Headquarters. Candidates whose applications are accepted are called for a written exam followed by an interview conducted by a preliminary interview board (PIB). Selected candidates go through the SSB interview, medical board and police verification. Candidates who are finally successful in their applications are granted commissions by the President of India. All officers have to undergo ten weeks of post-commission training within two years of being commissioned. All TA officers have to serve a minimum of two months in the year and during this period, they are entitled to the same pay, allowances, canteen and other benefits given to regular Army officers.

The TA is a part of the regular Indian Army. TA units are commanded by regular Army officers of Colonel rank who oversee training of officers and soldiers and whatever responsibilities come their way. The Territorial Army is meant to relieve the regular Army from static duties and also come forward in times of natural calamities to assist the civil administration. Its duties include maintenance of essential services in situations where the lives of citizens are affected in any way or when the security of the country is threatened. It also provides units to the regular Army as and when required.

Major Mohanlal (the film star), Lieutenant Colonel Kapil Dev and Lieutenant Colonel M.S. Dhoni (cricketers) are three of our honorary TA officers, who have been conferred these ranks in recognition of their service in their fields.

21

'There's no promotion for disabled soldiers.'

Myth—Disabled soldiers do not get promoted in the Army.
Reality—Major General S.K. Razdan (Retd.), KC, 7 PARA,
India's first General in a wheelchair.

8 November, 1994
Naugam village
Jammu and Kashmir

It is a dark and cold night when a crack team led by Lieutenant
Colonel Sunil Kumar Razdan, in a thick phiran and a black
patka, goes looking for a militant hideout in Kashmir. He and
his team of twenty handpicked men, dressed in phirans to
blend in with the locals, are on a search-and-destroy mission.
They have been told that nine Lashkar-e-Taiba militants
have kidnapped fourteen women from the Qazigund area,
including Rehana, the fourteen-year-old daughter of the

compounder at the primary health centre who has approached the Army for help. Razdan and his men have been tasked with rescuing them.

It is Razdan's birthday and also the third day of his Navratri fast. Yet he has walked for fifteen hours with his men, mostly over mountainous terrain along the ridge line, to cover forty kilometres and reach the outskirts of Naugam. It is 9.30 p.m. and the hungry soldiers light up a fire to make themselves some khichdi. They are carrying rice and buy some potatoes from the village. A Kashmiri Pandit, Razdan can speak three dialects of Kashmiri, which helps him converse with villagers and find out that the militants are holed up in an old house in a hamlet near a mountain spring about one-and-a-half kilometres away. After finishing dinner, the men walk another hour to reach the location. There are three to four houses in that area. The militants were in a big house with a massive compound that has a boundary wall running around it. The soldiers are carrying raw meat, which they throw across to the local dogs to keep them from barking. The rest of the team stealthily surrounds the house while Razdan and six others go in. 'As taught in our room intervention drill, out of the six, two went to the first floor, two remained outside the main door and two entered the house with me,' now Maj Gen S.K. Razdan (Retd.) remembers.

'By the light of a single oil lamp burning there, I saw thirteen women, from fourteen to thirty-five years of age, clustered together in a room. Then I noticed there was one more lady making omelettes in the kitchen. She was the first to spot me and, mistaking me for a militant, started screaming.

I quietly assured her that I was from the Army and opening the front door, told her to escape to safety along with the others,' he says. The women start wailing with relief and that, combined with the sounds of their jangling anklets, alerts the militants. Two of them rush down from the first floor but Razdan, who is expecting it, quickly shoots them down.

He spots a third militant coming down the stairs and fires a burst at him with his AK-47. The man tumbles down the steps and falls on top of the two dead men with his face up, his gun still in his hands. Presuming him to be dead, Razdan steps past the bodies to leave the house, hoping to join the rest of his men who have cordoned off the house. Unfortunately, that is not to be. The militant, who is still alive, empties ten bullets in Razdan's stomach at close range, splitting it open and making his intestines spill out. Razdan fires a retaliatory burst but his spine has broken and he falls. 'I had to unravel the patka around my head and tie it tightly around my stomach to keep my intestines in,' he says. He then crawls out of the house, dragging along four guns, leaving a trail of blood. 'I knew right then that I would never walk again.'

The firefight rages through the night with Razdan watching from behind a shack of stored firewood. He finds a vein and injects himself with a saline solution to keep from dehydrating and passing out. It is only after all nine militants are shot down that he agrees to be moved. He is airlifted to the Srinagar General Hospital from where he is taken to Delhi. Nine feet of his small intestine has to be removed. After he has recovered, he is again airlifted to Military Hospital, Khadki, Pune, for his rehabilitation. The villagers of Naugam village are so grateful to him for what he has done that they keep following his progress. They visit him even at Pune where they give Rs 10,000 to his wife that they have collected in the village. A few years later in Delhi, a Kashmiri Muslim selling shawls outside Razdan's bungalow recognizes him as the hero of Naugam and comes in to gift him a shawl that he absolutely refuses to take payment for. 'That was the respect Kashmiri Muslims gave me,' he says, 'They were so grateful to me for saving their women.'

This act of incredible bravery wins him the Kirti Chakra, the second-highest peacetime gallantry award, but leaves him paralysed for life. The General admits he faced a period of intense depression and darkness more dense than the night he had led that daring operation in, while lying on his hospital bed, wondering what life would be like without legs. But he came out of it with his head held high. 'I had a responsibility towards my wife, children and my country. The one thing I did not want from anyone was pity,' he says. He did very well professionally, moving from one promotion to another. 'I kept doing my job well and with complete sincerity. The promotions just came to me. I never had to struggle for them,' he says.

General Razdan is sixty-two now. He has retired from the Army in 2012 and lives in a Gurgaon flat. He says he is losing muscle with age and makes sure he exercises his arms every morning using weights tied to a three-brick pulley slung around the trunk of a tree in his front yard. He lives with a twenty-four-hour neural pain that he says feels as if he is standing on a burning hot plate all the time. He sleeps on his face to avoid bed sores but they still happen; his skin has become very delicate and cuts don't heal easily. 'It's tough,' he says, 'but I have no regrets in life and I won't give up. Physical disability is never as serious as being mentally disabled. If you are mentally mobile, you can do almost anything in life.'

The man who used to be a mountaineer, who went on a motorcycle expedition from Agra to Bengaluru when he was young and patrolled the jungles of Manipur, where he survived on python meat roasted on bamboo sticks, can no longer stand without using his walker. But the feisty paratrooper's spirit remains undaunted. Watch him moving his wheelchair around with the ease of a practised rally driver and you know that he is still the adventurous biker who once did Delhi–Agra in two hours on his Bullet motorcycle and was called Greyhound by his friends for his addiction to long-distance running. His enthusiasm remains the same; only the scope of his activities has changed. General Razdan and some of his course mates are involved in a social project where they identify children of Army widows and adopt them, taking full responsibility of their education. At one time he saved lives, now he is making a difference to them.

Institutions

Here are some premier Army institutions that you might not have heard about. They are the best in their field and have consistently been providing the country with some of its best professionals.

The National Defence Academy

The National Defence Academy (NDA), located at Khadakwasla, about seventeen kilometres away from Pune, is the joint services academy of the Indian Armed Forces. It happens to be the first tri-service academy of the world, where cadets of all three services, the Army, the Navy and the Air Force, train together. After graduating from the NDA, officers are sent to train at the service academies of the Army, Navy and Air Force, depending on which force they have opted for. Very few people know that the NDA is the first tri-service academy in the world.

The NDA campus is breathtakingly beautiful, spread over 7,015 acres of land. The site was picked for the Academy because it was on the banks of the Khadakwasla Lake. It also has a lot of area that can be utilized in the training of cadets. Its proximity to the Arabian Sea and other military establishments like the nearby air base at Lohegaon helps make it a perfect training ground. An out-of-service ship, *HMS Angostura*, anchored on the north bank of the Khadakwasla Lake, has been in use for training cadets for amphibious landings over many years.

The Sudan Block is a magnificent three-storey basalt and granite building that functions as the administrative headquarter of the Academy. The foyer has white Italian marble flooring and on its walls are the awe-inspiring portraits of NDA graduates who went on to win the highest awards—the Param Vir Chakra and the Ashoka Chakra. A number of war relics can be found all over the NDA campus. These include tanks and aircraft captured during wars. The beautiful library—aptly termed Vyas Library—has a collection of over 1,00,000 printed volumes, electronic subscriptions as well as those to a number of periodicals and journals from around the world in at least ten languages.

The UPSC conducts a written entrance exam for the NDA that is counted amongst the toughest institutions in the world to get into. This is followed by interviews and physicals conducted by the SSB. A young boy wanting to join the Armed Forces is tested for general aptitude, psychology, team skills, physical and social behaviour and physical well-being. The terms start in July and January. About 4,50,000 applicants sit for each written exam and approximately 6,300 are called for the interview. Only 320 cadets are accepted to the academy each semester. These include about seventy cadets for the Air Force, forty-two for the Navy and 208 for the Army. All candidates should have cleared Class XII or its equivalent exams from a well-recognized board. Candidates appearing for these exams can also apply.

On successful completion of the three-year course, Army cadets go to Dehradun, to the IMA, Naval cadets to the Indian Naval Academy in Ezhimala and Air Force cadets to the Air Force Academy in Hyderabad. After one year of training at their respective academies, cadets are commissioned as officers into the respective services. The Academy also trains cadets from allied foreign countries.

The Indian Military Academy

The Indian Military Academy, which has given the Indian Army some of its finest officers, was established in 1932. It is located in the foothills of the Himalayas, about eight kilometres west of Dehradun in Uttarakhand. It is spread out over an area of 1,400 acres.

The IMA was built in 1930. Its most famous building is the Chetwode Hall on the Drill Square which serves as the administrative headquarters of the IMA and is also the place where classes are conducted. It has lecture halls, computer labs and a café. On the opposite side of the Drill Square is the Khetarpal Auditorium, named after the famous 1971 war hero, Second Lieutenant Arun Khetarpal, Param Vir Chakra, one of the youngest awardees of the PVC. Arun died in his burning tank soon after he refused to evacuate after it had been hit in the war. Inaugurated in 1982, the auditorium seats 2,000.

A newer wing was added to the Chetwode Hall in 1938. It houses the Central Library, which is a treat for the intellectually inclined. Not only does the library boast of more than 100,000 volumes, it also subscribes to hundreds of periodicals from across the world. There is an IMA Museum also on the campus that showcases artefacts of historic importance. One of its most famous war relics is the pistol of Lieutenant General Amir Abdullah Khan Niazi of the Pakistani Army. This is the same weapon that he surrendered to Lieutenant General Jagjit Singh Aurora after signing the Instrument of Surrender to end the 1971 war.

One of the most beautiful buildings in the Academy is the Commandant's residence. Its colonial architecture is eye-catching. The IMA also has a helipad which is located in the Tons Valley in the north-west of the campus, stables with a stud farm, a small arms shooting range and even a polo ground that runs along the Tons river. The Tons Valley is used for para-dropping, para-gliding and also battle training.

All trainees who join the IMA are referred to as Gentleman Cadets. It is a way of reiterating to them that they are expected to uphold the highest ethics and moral values. GCs are expected to draw inspiration from an excerpt from a speech by Field Marshal Chetwode that is inscribed at the eastern entrance of the Chetwode Hall. It is what he said at the inauguration of the Academy in 1932:

'The safety, honour and welfare of your country come first, always and every time.

The honour, welfare and comfort of the men you command come next.

Your own ease, comfort and safety come last, always and every time.'

The Officers Training Academy

The Officers Training Academy is a premier institute of the Indian Army that trains officers who opt for SSC. The Academy is located in Chennai amidst a sprawling estate of 650 acres traversed by the Adyar river.

The difference between IMA and OTA is that IMA trains men for permanent commissions while those who opt for SSC (which means they have the option to leave after serving a specific number of years) are trained at the OTA. When women were invited to join the Indian Army as commissioned officers, the OTA started training them as well. The first batch of twenty-five women officers was trained by OTA in 1992.

The history of the OTA dates back to World War II, when seven officer training institutes were established in India. However, these schools were closed down after the war. In 1962, after the war with China, India felt the need to train more officers for the Indian Army. Two officers' training schools were established, one in Chennai and the other in Pune. These officer training schools (OTSs) were established with the aim of training officers for emergency commissions. While Pune was later shut down, Chennai continued to train soldiers. When the emergency commission courses were discontinued, the OTS started training GCs for SSCs. In the 1970s, the OTS underwent many infrastructural developments. A swimming pool, an auditorium, a science block and laboratories, a Drill Square, Cadets Mess, weapon-training sheds were created to facilitate the training of GCs.

On 1 January 1988, as a part of its silver jubilee celebrations, the Officers Training School was renamed the Officers Training Academy. The forty-nine-week course at the Academy prepares graduates for all the branches of the Army. In 2011, a new OTA was also set up at Gaya.

The College of Military Engineering

The College of Military Engineering (CME) in Pune is where the Army trains its engineer officers. A premier technical and tactical training institution of the Indian Army Corps of Engineers, the CME was established in 1943 as the School of Military Engineering (SME) at Roorkee. Later, it was moved to Pune. The CME offers young officers the option of doing BTech courses in civil, electrical and mechanical engineering.

The college trains officers from the Indian Army and friendly countries. It is also majorly involved in research projects and plays an advisory role to the Indian Army. Affiliated to Jawaharlal Nehru University, the College of Military Engineering offers both BTech and MTech degrees. Corps of EME and Signal officers also complete the first three semesters of their BTech degree from CME.

The lush green CME campus is situated on the banks of the Mula river and spread over 3,600 acres. It includes the sparkling CME Lake, Sarvatra Bir, a bird sanctuary, Harkirat Singh Theatre, an open-air theatre that screens the latest releases from Hollywood as well as Bollywood and serves samosas too, a shopping complex, a concert hall, an Officers' Institute with a bar, a restaurant and a dance floor. The campus also caters to accommodation for students and teachers, and their families.

Army Air Defence College

The Army Air Defence College (AADC) is a major training academy for officers of the Army Air Defence Corps of the Indian Army. It educates officers about air defence systems and anti-aircraft warfare. Training is offered to officers from the Army, Navy and Air Force as well as from friendly foreign countries. The college is in Gopalpur, Odisha, with a lush campus spread over 2700 acres of land.

The Armed Forces Medical College

Not only do the Armed Forces have their own engineers and pilots, they also have their own doctors. These doctor soldiers are trained at the Armed Forces Medical College (AFMC) at Pune. The college was established in 1962, soon after World War II, on the recommendation of the B.C. Roy Committee. The college came into being on combining whatever remained of different Indian Army Medical Corps units. AFMC Day is celebrated on 4 August 1962. The date is important because it marks the day that the AFMC undergraduate wing was established.

AFMC is counted amongst the top medical colleges of India. It ranked second amongst all the undergraduate medical institutions of the country as per a survey done by *Outlook* magazine in 2012 and again in 2015. The Institution has been providing a pool of 'doctor soldiers' to the Armed Forces year after year. Entrance is through the common all-India medical entrance test.

How Do I Join the Army?

You can be an engineer, a lawyer, a cyber warrior, a mountaineer, a skydiver, a paratrooper, an Olympian and also an Army officer. The Army has a wide range of jobs and opportunities you can apply for. If you think you would like to join the Army, take a look at this.

Qualifications and entry schemes

So now you know that an Army officer is not always a guy with a gun. Once you join the Army, you have the choice of opting for what you would like to be. You could join the infantry if a regular soldier's role impresses you, you could pick Army Aviation if you would like to fly a helicopter to work; you could join the engineers if you wish to be a Sapper officer; you could join the Judge Advocate General's branch if a lawyer is what you wish to be. You could also opt for being a paratrooper or join the Special Forces. If adventure interests you, you could approach the Army Adventure Wing and register your name for a mountaineering expedition or skydiving or white-water rafting. If you have Olympic dreams, you could look up Mission Olympics. It's a career that will never let you get bored.

Entry schemes for men

Men can join the Army after 10 +2, after graduation, after doing a professional degree like engineering, law and so on. Women can join the Army only after graduation or after a professional degree. For more details on Entry Schemes for Men, please see: https://joinindianarmy.nic.in/alpha/entry-schemes-men.htm.

Entry schemes for women

In 1992, an important landmark in the history of the Indian Army was the induction of women into the officer cadre, and the onerous task of training them was undertaken by the OTA. So far, more than 1,200 lady officers have already been commissioned into the various Arms and Services of the Indian Army. You should be a graduate to apply.

For details: https://joinindianarmy.nic.in/alpha/entry-schemes-women.htm.

If you have decided you would like to be an Army officer, here is a chart showing you the various options open to you.

COMMISSIONED OFFICERS

SER No.	COURSE/ ENTRY	ELIGIBILITY CRITERIA		TRAINING ACADEMY	DURATION OF TRAINING
		AGE	QUALIFICATIONS		
1.	NDA	16 ½ to 19 ½ years (As on the first day of the month in which course is due to commence)	12th class of 10+2 equivalent for Army and with Physics and Maths for Air Force and Navy	NDA Khadakwasla, Pune	3 years at NDA and 1 year at IMA
2.	10+2 (TES)	16 ½ to 19 ½ years (As on the first day of the month in which course is due to commence)	10+2 Physics, Chemistry and Maths (aggregate 70% and above to apply)	OTA, Gaya	5 years (1 year at OTA, Gaya and 4 years at CTWS). Permanent Commission after 4 years as under:- Phase-I. 1 year Pre-Commissioning Training at OTA, Gaya and 3 years at CME Pune/MCTE Mhow/ MCEME Sexunderabad Phase-II. 1 year Post-Commissioning Training at CME Pune/MCTE Mhow/ MCEME Secunderabad
3.	IMA (DE)	19 to 24 years (As on the first day of the month in which course is due to commence)	Graduate from recognized University	IMA, Dehradun	1 ½ years
4.	SSC (NT) (Men and Women)	19 to 25 years (As on 1st Jan of the year for Apr course and as on 1st July of the year for Oct course)	Graduate from a recognized University	OTA, Chennai	49 weeks
5.	NCC (SPL Entry) (Men and Women)	19 to 25 years (As on 1st Jan of the year for Apr course and on 1st July of the year for Oct course)	Graduation with 50% aggregate marks, 2 years service in NCC Sr. Div Army Wing with minimum 'B' grade in NCC 'C' Certificate Exam	OTA, Chennai	49 weeks
6.	SSC (JAG) (Men and Women)	21 to 27 years (As on 1st Jan of the year for Apr course and on 1st July of the year for Oct course)	Graduate with LLB 55% marks. Elligible to enroll as Advocate in Bar Council of India/States	OTA, Chennai	49 weeks
7.	UES	18 to 24 years (As on the first day of the month in which course is due to commence) Enrollment in local colleges, 2005	Pre-final year students of BE/B. Tech Course of the notified streams	IMA, Dehradun	1 year
8.	TGC	20 to 27 years (As on the first day of the month in which course is due to commence)	BE/B. Tech in notified streams	IMA, Dehradun	1 year
9.	SSC (Tech) (Men and Women)	20 to 27 years (As on the first day of the month in which course is due to commence)	BE/B. Tech in notified streams	OTA, Chennai	49 weeks
10.	AEC	23 to 27 years (As on the first day of the month in which course is due to commence)	Post Graduate in 1st or 2nd division in notified subjects from recognized University	OTA, Chennai	1 year

For complete details and information on the various entry schemes to the Indian Army, please visit: http://joinindianarmy.nic.in/index.htm.

Acknowledgements

I would like to begin by acknowledging the twenty-one absolutely awesome Army officers—ladies and gentlemen—living and serving across the vast expanse of our country, from Sikkim to Siachen, who took the time out of their busy schedules to have lunch, coffee and conversation with me over the year that it took to write *Shoot. Dive. Fly*. Thank you for sharing your amazing stories with me.

I am grateful to my team of teenage critics: senior school students Isha Pareek, Samiha Khajuria, Arundhati Kale, Shashwat Aggarwal, Siddharth Balyan, Siddhant Banerjee and Saransh Rawat, who meticulously read the initial few chapters and gave me feedback on the right tone for the stories. Saransh helped all the way through—from the writing of the book to cover design. (He charged me for it in Sony headphones too!)

I would also like to thank Colonel Grewal and his team of officers at the Additional Directorate General of Public Information (ADGPI), Indian Army, for giving me access to serving officers and logistical support. Without those endless brainstorming sessions and permissions, this book couldn't have been written.

Then there are my editors at Penguin Random House—Sohini Mitra (always the picture of composed calm, even when I suspected she was secretly tearing her hair out) and Anupam Kant Verma, who stepped in to read the manuscript first and rapped me on the knuckles (gently) where he felt stories slacked. I would also like to thank Niyati Dhuldhoya. She is one of the most meticulous copy-editors I have worked with and has contributed a lot towards making this a humbler book, and me a better person, by stomping really hard on my ego and making me redo large sections.

Shoot. Dive. Fly. is a fun book written with a serious objective—to introduce the Indian Army as an exciting career option to young people which I hope will help fill up the shortfall in the officer cadre that the Army faces year after year. If this book manages to interest Gen Next enough to consider a career in olive-greens, that will be my greatest reward. Thank you for reading it.

I'm grateful to Lt Ranjith who requested his fellow paratrooper Lt Col M.S. Dhoni to give us a foreword for the book and to M.S. Dhoni for his immense generosity in agreeing at once and for mailing a signed copy to me.